Boredom Busters

Themed Special Events to Dazzle and Delight Your Group

Boredom Busters

Themed Special Events to Dazzle and Delight Your Group

by Annette C. Moore
illustrated by Dennis Perry

Venture Publishing, Inc.
State College, Pennsylvania

Venture Publishing, Inc.
1999 Cato Avenue
State College, PA 16801
Phone (814) 234-4561
Fax (814) 234-1651

Production Manager: Richard Yocum
Manuscript Editing: Valerie Fowler, Richard Yocum

Library of Congress Catalogue Card Number 2004111881
ISBN 1-892132-52-4

Dedication

This book is dedicated to all of you investing your lives in service to others. Through the recreation programs you offer, you are touching people's lives, making the world a better and happier place to live for all of us. *Thank you* for making a positive difference in individuals' lives, in your communities, and in our society.

So then let us pursue the things which make for peace and the building up of one another. (Romans 14:19)

Acknowledgments

My name may be the only one listed as the author of this book, but many people contributed to its successful completion. My family not only provided endless encouragement while I wrote, they served in some capacity on nearly every leadership team for these events. They brainstormed ideas, assembled props, tested games, counted candies, lead activities, greeted guests, even served as MC when needed. Thank you, Roger, Sarah, and Marinna! You are my greatest treasures on this earth. I love you!

I am grateful to my church family at Triangle Vineyard Christian Fellowship, who willingly and joyously served as guinea pigs for many of these events. Thank you for all your encouragement and for helping with so many Kids Nights Out and Family Fun Nights. Special thanks to Joe, Bev, Rebecca, and Natalie Sarver (a born leader), Dave and Cindy Pletcher, and Ken and Sharon Martin for countless hours of effort and creative support. It is wonderful to serve with you all and to learn so much by watching you be you. How good and how pleasant it is for brethren to dwell together in unity, and to spur one another on to love and good deeds. Thank you for your faithful friendship and help with this project!

A big thank you to my friend and illustrator, Dennis Perry. Your creative ideas and talents have brought such life to these pages—and to our lives. Thank you for sharing your talents, life, and family with us!

Even from afar, my mom, Helen Cardenuto, has been such a source of encouragement and support throughout this project. Actually, throughout my life. Thank you for all the gentle inquiries about my progress, Mom. I sure hope I can be half as good a mom to my girls as you have been, and continue to be, for me!

What a gift God has given me in family and friends and in the ability to facilitate fun for folks! To Him be the glory.

Table of Contents

Introduction

Ever feel bored? You feel like doing something, but nothing is particularly appealing? It's sort of like looking into a full refrigerator or cupboard and concluding, "There's nothing good to eat in this house!" For a good number of people, life is a lot like that. They work hard at jobs, at school, and even with their families. Yet, they seem to have no zest in their lives. They may not know what they want, but they know what they are doing for leisure is not particularly satisfying. It's important for us to remember the opposite of boredom isn't merely "being occupied"—it's excitement. That's what the programs and special events in this book strive for—*excitement!* People who are bored with life are not going to be satisfied with being occupied with a "nice" program. They can sit home, watch TV, and be occupied without any effort at all. (Of course, they are not likely to feel much satisfaction from that.) What they really want is to feel alive. They want excitement. They want to feel involved and important. They want to be the star of the show. So let's plan programs that are innovative and exciting. Let's get people off the couch and into our facilities. Let's transform them into superheroes or game show contestants, even if for just an hour or two. Let's remind them how satisfying having fun can be!

Boredom Busters: Themed Special Events to Dazzle and Delight Your Group was created to assist you in bringing some excitement to the lives of those you serve. I believe this book will be a very valuable tool for you as you prepare social recreation programs for your group. I have designed *Boredom Busters* to be very straightforward, so you can easily see the steps and considerations involved in delivering creative programs. If you have a need for great programs, yet have little time to develop them yourself, I've designed this book to provide you with lots of ready-to-go plans. These creative (dare I say, crazy!) events are sure to give even the most hardened couch potatoes a lift! You are working hard to provide quality services to your clientele. *Boredom Busters* is here to help you!

Boredom Busters contains two main sections. Program Planning Procedures are explained in Section 1. Particulars concerning what you need to do to organize, plan, and run a successful themed special event as well as leadership skills and tips to maximize the positive impacts you have on your participants are discussed. This section was designed to give you sufficient background information and ideas to help you get ready to run exciting social recreation events.

Section 2 showcases 15 preplanned themed special events. Included in these chapters are lists of activities, props, and leadership tips, and a checklist for each theme program. You can pick programs that are suitable for children, adults or mixed groups, and ones for high energy or more sedate participation. Read through all the events; see which ones strike you, and which will best work with your group. Use your professional judgment and knowledge of your participants to create the ultimate themed event for your group.

My primary goal for writing this book is to help you to successfully run creative programs. I want you to be effective as a program planner. I want your participants to come up to you after an event and say, "I had a really great time! I am so glad I came!" Sure, there is a lot of planning and coordination that goes into successful events. You don't always have the luxury of a lot of planning time. That's one reason I created *Boredom Busters*. Much of the planning has been done for you here already, so you can focus on taking these plans and making them happen.

Remember, the more programs you plan and run, the more confident and capable you will become. As you continue to present creative and exciting programs, your clientele will enjoy the benefits of social recreation, which can create a wonderful ripple effect throughout your whole community and to our whole society. The television advertisers may not be thrilled you got some folks off the couch and into your fun activities. But just think of the difference you are making in the lives of the individuals and the families who attend! Creative program planning is definitely worth the effort.

Thanks for picking up *Boredom Busters*. I can't wait for you to get started! You've got some great programs in your hands, just waiting to be implemented. You've got some great ideas in your head, just waiting to be realized. And you've got some great people in your community, just waiting to be touched with the excitement and joy these themed special events can provide.

Let's get started!

Section 1

Program Planning Procedures

Chapter 1

An Overview
of Themed Special Events

Themed special events make for magical memories. Shared events, especially ones which are delightfully fun, develop a unity among participants. People who cooperate to achieve a common goal create a bond that transcends differences. And that bond lasts longer than the event itself. "Wasn't that fun?" "Remember when this happened?" Memories of the event and the joyful interactions linger long after the program has ended.

Through themed special events, you have the opportunity to make positive impacts in the lives of all the people who attend. Everyone needs to feel they are a valued part of a group. Your event has the potential of transforming a collection of individuals into a cohesive team. You can create a sense of value and belonging for your participants. And they'll have a great time doing it, as well!

The Value of a Theme

Each of the special events outlined in this book revolves around a separate theme. A theme gives a gathering more focus. When carried through in every aspect of the event, a theme can give an event an incredible air of delight, wonder, and excitement. The more you can develop and carry that theme through, the more you can create a unique, often magical, atmosphere. The sights, sounds, smells, textures, and tastes of an event combine to transport a participant from the everyday to the extraordinary. A familiar gymnasium is no longer ordinary when you transform it into an inviting summer beach scene by setting up beach umbrellas, towels, and beach chairs. Create a sandy beach for castle building. Don Hawaiian shirts and slather on aromatic cocoa butter. Fill the air with Beach Boys tunes. Indeed, the participant feels he or she has entered into an extravagant affair designed expressly for his or her enjoyment when attention to detail is demonstrated in a well-executed theme event.

People like to feel special, as if someone went all-out for them. We certainly want our participants to feel special, if for no other reason than to make them more likely to return for future events. One way we can do this is by selecting a theme for each event, and carrying that theme through as much as possible. (More about themes in Chapter 2.)

Definition of Terms

Before we get any farther into our discussion of planning themed special events, we need to define the terms that will be used. Throughout this book, the term *themed special event* will mean a one-time social recreation gathering centered around a particular theme. Each themed special event is comprised of various activities. These activities are often games, though some are merely fun things that can be done by individuals or groups in a noncompetitive manner. Games are often competitive, and may involve teams (e.g., relay races) or the whole group (e.g., tag). *Program* is a more encompassing word, which in our case will usually refer to the one-time themed special event, although it could also refer to a series of special events or other recreational gatherings.

Why Are We Doing This?

Before you begin planning your themed special event, consider why you are hosting it. Are you trying to build group cohesion? Do you want to celebrate a special occasion? Is there a "message" you want to convey in a fun and creative way? Take time at the onset to think about and articulate what the purpose of your event is. Clearly state your objectives. They will provide direction, aid in making decisions, and serve as a means for evaluation. If one of your expressed purposes is to build a sense of community among participants, you will move in that direction, selecting activities that positively bond group members together rather than single out people as potential activity winners or losers. As participants interact socially at the conclusion of your event, your observations should confirm a sense of community has grown through participation in your event. Without stated objectives, your programs are "hit or miss" in making a positive difference in your participants. The activities may be pleasant enough, but the whole package may lack the real, positive impact you could potentially be making. Think about what you would like to accomplish through this event, and communicate that clearly throughout your leadership team. If we all understand the purpose of our event, we can all work together to make sure we accomplish it.

One of the standing objectives for your events should be to present programs with a customer service orientation. Simply put, a customer service orientation recognizes the value of the people who are our customers. Because we value them highly, our participants are to be treated with respect and courtesy, and consciously served as honored guests in our midst. While this may sound a bit contrived on paper, people are worthy of being treated in this positive manner—regardless of the recognition, prestige, or money they may bring to our agency. As citizens of the world we should be affirming others. Our themed special events provide us with a highly conducive avenue for doing so. Please adopt a customer service attitude when conducting your events, and train your staff to do so as well.

Consider additional objectives for your events related to

- family bonding.

- forming a sense of community.

- broadening horizons.

- a sense of physical and mental engagement.

- affirmation of self and of others.

- celebrating community identity and diversity.

- creating opportunities for laughter to break down barriers.

Structure of Leadership in Themed Special Events

The leadership of an event is critical to its success. Planning and running special events is not a job for a "Lone Ranger." While one person does need to be ultimately responsible for the coordination of an event, "many hands make for light work" and for a better product.

The overall leader of the themed special event is the *Event Coordinator*. This person makes sure everything that needs to be done is getting accomplished, the goals of the program are being realized, and the people needed to run the event are trained and ready to go. Since you have picked up this book and are interested in planning and running themed special events, I will consider you, the reader, the Event Coordinator for the events you are planning.

Working with the Event Coordinator should be a *Leadership Team*. This group's purpose is to assist with the planning and preparations for the event, as well as to play primary leadership roles during the event itself. Most likely, the leadership team will consist of adults or older youth. Depending on your group and your particular situation, you may want to involve some members of your target population in the leadership team. By planning with members of your target population, you will get "expert" input on what will and won't work for this particular group. They can also be excellent promoters for your event. They know it will be a super event—they helped plan it! Your leadership team may include paid *Staff Members* and *Volunteers*, depending on your individual situation. The more complex your event and the larger the number of participants, the larger you will want your leadership team to be. Generally, five to nine people in addition to yourself are ideal for groups of 50 to 80. Allow for an additional leader for about every 10 participants over that. Members of the leadership team may also serve as game leaders or judges during the program, as needed.

You will want to recruit more people to serve as assistants during the actual event. Depending on the nature of your themed special event, some or all of the following assistants may be needed to make your event go more smoothly. In general, the younger the participants or the more complex the event, the more assistants you will want to have on hand. Some key assistant positions are listed next.

A *Master of Ceremonies* plays a critical role in the success of your event. Like the ringmaster at a circus, the Master of Ceremonies (MC) is the focal person during the welcome and dismissal. She or he regulates the tone and the tempo of the event. This person serves as the main leader in the eyes of the participants. As the Event Coordinator, you may want to take on this role if you feel comfortable doing so and have the skills needed to be enthusiastic yet instructive in front of a crowd. This person's role is critical for managing the event, keeping the event moving along, and monitoring the emotional climate of the group.

Game Leaders are responsible for giving directions to the entire group, demonstrating how a game is run, monitoring the game, and declaring "winners." They may be assisted by *Judges*, if the particular activity requires them, or if the Game Leaders want help in determining first, second, and third place winners. Judges may also be helpful in determining whether a team has performed a task adequately.

The *Props Crew* move in any props needed for each game, and move out the ones previously used. Needless to say, these folks are essential to the smooth transition between activities. For a themed special event like "Game Show Gala," you will want a team of people whose sole responsibility is being the Props Crew. For less complex events, the Leadership Team could rotate into this function.

A *Scorekeeper* is an essential team member for events that will include a lot of relay races. On a large sheet of posterboard, or overhead transparency, the Scorekeeper keeps track of how many points each team receives for each race. By having a designated Scorekeeper, the Game Leader can keep the activities moving without having to stop and record scores.

The *Candy Meister* is an optional position. If you choose to reward teams in a confectionery way, the Candy Meister will put candy in bags for each team that wins a race. If you prefer, inexpensive candy can be placed in each participant's bag, and "better" candy can be inserted as teams win a race. Since relays are often pretty quick activities, a designated Candy Meister should be responsible for this important task. Of course, you don't have to give candy. You could give other trinket-y prizes, or simply have a theme-related prize for the winning team. Personally, I like going home with some sort of prize or treat, so I feel like a winner regardless of the total points my team earned.

For some themed special events, you may want to recruit an *Announcer*. This person should be comfortable with public speaking—especially in a spontaneous manner. This person could also be in charge of playing the background music while participants arrive

and during the active games. He or she may
also want to give periodic updates of the teams'
rankings, or interject comments to keep the
crowd excited about your event. For many of the
events in this book, the Master of Ceremonies
can easily fill this role.

Team Coaches are extremely
helpful if your program involves youngsters or a lot of relays. Team coaches should have
a good understanding of what
is involved in each activity, so
they can facilitate their team's efforts effectively. Team
coaches are also responsible for maintaining control
of their team, and recruiting team representatives if a
particular game needs only one or a few players from
each team. Depending on your group, you may need
to provide these leaders or designate a parent or staff
member to fill this role. With older groups, you may recruit a team
member to serve.

Greeters play a vital role in setting the tone for your themed special event. As your guests arrive, these greeters personally welcome
each person, sign them in, issue nametags, and instruct participants
where to proceed. If parents are dropping off their children, these
greeters can get any necessary information or signatures and assure
parents of the care their children will receive. These Greeters should
also be responsible for reuniting children with their respective care-
givers following the event.

Safety Monitors should keep an eye out for anything that could
be a potential hazard. Spilled water may make a tile floor very slippery, for example. A child may need to use the bathroom, which may
be in a different part of your building and require an escort. A skinned
knee may need to be tended. While safety should be everyone's business, it is wise to have a person or two designated to specifically monitor safety before and during the event.

Now that you have a basic foundation of what a themed special
event is and the leadership team needed to plan and run it, let's move
on to some particulars about organizing your event.

Chapter 2

Organizing Your Event

Taking time to organize your themed special event is essential to providing high quality experiences in a safe setting. The more events you plan and run, the more natural it will be to you. In this chapter, we look at the key components of planning a themed special event.

Selecting a Leadership Team

As we discussed in the last chapter, having a team of leaders to plan and run your event is imperative for success. The leadership team may be made up of members of your paid staff, adults who have a vested interest in the target population, and members of the target population itself. While individual skills and abilities may vary, each team member should be willing to serve and to give the time, energy, and enthusiasm required to plan and execute the event. Be clear in communicating the time and effort requirements to potential team members. Once they understand your request, they will likely be self-selecting in volunteering to serve. In addition, you should clearly articulate your objectives for the event and for impacting your guests in a positive manner. Approach people you believe can help you achieve these goals and represent your agency professionally.

Planning Steps

Advanced planning is fundamental to a well-run special event. Pages 10 and 11 offer general guidelines for you to follow. By utilizing the preplanned themed special events found in this book, you should be able to prepare for your event easily. Each event includes a detailed list of what you need to make, purchase, or gather, and assistants you need to recruit. Please read the entire series of steps, and modify to meet your needs if necessary.

Step 1

- Recruit leadership team members.

- Determine the objectives for the event.

- Set date and location for the event.

- Select a themed special event. Consider which would be most appropriate for your group, your agency, and your objectives.

Step 2

- Assign members of the leadership team to be in charge of different aspects of the program. These assignments might include promotions and registration, decorations and refreshments, game leadership, facilities, props, and music.

- Develop a timeline for organizing and running your event.

- Distribute copies of the agreed timeline and individual responsibilities to leadership team members.

Step 3

- Advertise to the target market and begin taking registrations.

- Recruit additional assistants to serve in leadership support roles, such as Announcer and Scorekeeper.

- Review selected activities for safety and appropriateness.

- Assign someone to lead each of the activities.

- Begin making and gathering props for the event.

- Determine how the selected facility can best be utilized for the event and what physical resources are available to you there (e.g., tables, chairs, open areas).

Step 4

- Practice leading the games with members of the leadership team. This will give the game leaders an opportunity to practice explaining the directions. This practice session will also give everyone a good understanding of how each activity is conducted and how the event flows.

- Modify activities as needed to match the participants' needs and abilities, watching out for and anticipating any safety issues.

Step 5

- Gather all props needed for the event.
- Set date for the final run through with whole team.
- Continue advertising efforts and registration.
- Finalize written directions sheets for each activity for the leadership team.
- Create a props "cheat sheet" listing each activity in order, what props each requires, and other related information (e.g., remove table and chairs, set out 12 bananas)

Step 6

- Hold final dress rehearsal of the event with entire leadership team. Include playing the games, so everyone knows how each activity is conducted.
- Acquire and organize prop supplies.
- Purchase refreshments.
- Prepare nametags for leadership team members and pre-registered guests.

Day of the Event

- Decorate and set up facility.

- Prepare registration table, group starters, refreshments table, and playing area.

- Arrange props in and out of the way yet easily accessible staging area.

- Gather your leadership team together for one final "pep talk" before the event, reminding them of the importance of their roles in facilitating a safe and enjoyable event for all present.

- Welcome your guests and enjoy your event!

After the Event

- Conduct evaluation of participant satisfaction.

- Evaluate the event with your staff during a postevent debrief.

- Return equipment.

- Write thank-you notes.

- Draft an evaluation summary of the event.

- Share photos and stories of your event with all participants through bulletin boards, newsletters, websites, and the media.

Theme Enhancers

As you plan your themed special event, consider how you can maximize the impact of the theme on your participants. Involve all five senses in your theme if you can. Decorations may be simple or elaborate, depending on your creativity and your resources. Decorations catch the participants' eyes as soon as they walk into your facility, and help set the tone for a delightful event. Have the staff and participants wear appropriate theme-related attire to the event. Not only does this provide visual stimulation, it gets the participants into the theme even before they arrive. Theme-related background music should be playing as guests arrive. Again, this builds excitement. If possible, allow

your participants to touch something related to the theme soon after they walk in, like bananas or beach balls. Group starters can be used in this way. What are the smells that could be associated with this event? Freshly popped popcorn, cocoa butter, and simmering spiced apple cider all emit tantalizing aromas that can help enhance a theme and captivate participants' senses! When the program is wrapping up, serve these aromatic treats and other theme-related goodies.

Physical Safety

Throughout your planning process, seek to minimize any potential safety problems. Consider the following three areas for minimizing potential risks.

Environmental Conditions

As you select a site for your event, consider what kinds of activities you might be conducting. Is there a smooth running surface? Is the area hazard free? Will you have adequate lighting? Is the temperature appropriate for the anticipated crowd? If the event will be held outdoors, what natural conditions might you need to consider (e.g., rain, poison ivy, excessive heat, insects)? Inspect the playing area for any protrusions, holes, or other hazardous spots. If these areas cannot be fixed, rope them off or otherwise barricade them to keep players out.

Depending on your setting, you may want to confine your players to one area of the facility. Partition off areas where you don't want people wandering. Supervision is essential for safety.

If your event will take place on a hard, smooth surface, be aware of the potential danger water can create. Activities involving liquids or semi-liquid substances (like gelatin or pudding), can create slippery spots on the floor. Make sure you have plenty of paper towels or rags on hand to immediately mop up any messes. Consider using a tarp taped to the floor for messy activities. When the game is over, you can roll up the tarp for cleaning later, and just wipe up any slippery spots.

The Activity Itself

Some activities are inherently dangerous and should not be part of your themed special event. Red Rover is one of those games that just begs for someone to get hurt. Don't risk injuring someone by choosing this type of activity.

Select activities appropriate for the age and ability levels of your participants. If you are leading a group of mixed ages or abilities, devise ways to modify the activity to accommodate the lowest level of ability, have only higher level players participate in this one activity, or scrap the activity and choose another.

Consider the props you are using for an activity. Select props which are as safe as possible. Avoid props that are sharp, could break easily, could be easily swallowed by young children, or that could be misused to produce injury for the player or others. Use professional judgment. Practice every activity so you can anticipate things that could go wrong. If you cannot remedy the potential problem, you should replace the activity with one that can be conducted safely for your group.

Supervising and Conducting the Activity

Make sure your leadership team has practiced every activity you will lead (see box, p. 15). This is the best way to anticipate any inherent dangers in the game or in how your participants may play it.

Give your game leader opportunities to practice describing and demonstrating the game. Make sure they are including appropriate safety precautions in the directions.

If any of the games involve eating, make sure participants are not moving while they have food in their mouths. Let them run to the food, eat the food, and show a judge they have finished swallowing their food, before heading back to their teammates. Pick judges with strong stomachs, if necessary, but don't skip this safety step.

Make sure your team coaches are watching their participants. Control any potentially disruptive behavior, stopping it before it gets out of hand. It is better to have one disruptive player removed from the game than to have players get hurt or to have the atmosphere of the event dampened to the dismay of all.

Our leadership team was nearing its final preparations for Friday's big event. We were practicing leading every game to make sure we could lead them well and had a good understanding of what our participants would be experiencing. Then we came to the Charleston Chew game. Seemed straightforward enough to all of us—players run to the center of the circle, munch down a candy bar quickly, judge checks the player's mouth to make sure food is swallowed before they run back to tag off the next player. We happened to use snack size bars for the kids, "lite" varieties for the ladies, and chilled regular sized bars for the men folk. None of us really wanted to consume the 240 calories or the 26 grams of fat, so we said, "We don't need to practice this one. Let's move on."

The night of the event we ran this game. All was going smoothly until one player jammed the candy bar in his mouth—and began choking! Fortunately, the judge for that team immediately recognized what was happening and administered the Heimlich maneuver, dislodging the candy bar. I don't think anyone else saw or knew what had just happened, but I have vowed never to lead an activity (especially one that involves eating food) that I haven't tested out, and never to use chilled candy bars for fast-eating contests.

Learn from my near-catastrophe: Practice EVERY activity with your leadership team before you present it to your group!

Emotional Safety

While it is very important to anticipate any hazards or risks which could injure our participants, it is equally important to consider emotional safety issues. Our participants are joining us for this themed special event because they are anticipating a positive experience. We need to design and conduct our programs to build up and encourage our participants. Certainly, people have many choices as to how to spend their time and money. If people have a wonderful experience, one in which they felt uplifted, they will likely return for another experience.

Each of the themed special events shared in this book have been designed with the participant in mind. As the activities progress, trust grows between the leadership team and team members. Excitement builds as teams work together to achieve common goals. As a leader, you need to encourage positive interactions among teams. Unlike professional sport teams, we feel the fun of playing the game is more important than winning or losing. As you review the games in each of the themed special events outlined in this book, you will notice I have purposely avoided activities meant to humiliate participants. The best games are the ones where everyone has a good time playing.

As participants play, recognize good efforts, positive attitudes, and team spirit in the group. Give high-fives and bonus points liberally to players and teams demonstrating positive attitudes. Do what you can to make each person feel like a winner.

Chapter 3

Getting Ready

You've got the leadership team and the ideas in place for your themed special event. As you near the day of your event, take some time to step out of the flow of activity to make sure you and your leadership team will be well-prepared. The effort you invest now will pay big dividends during your event.

Practice Sessions

Practice is essential to a successful themed special event. Through practice sessions, the game leaders gain experience in giving directions and demonstrations that are both entertaining and informative. The more they practice, the more confident they will feel, which will make the event more enjoyable for them—and those following the directions, too. It is through these practice sessions that the leadership team refines the activity and how to assist in its execution. Potentially dangerous aspects may also come to light, allowing you to avert them.

As the leadership team practices the activities you plan to do at your themed special event, they are able to distinguish between good games and boring ones. If the leadership team doesn't enjoy an activity, chances are good your participants won't either. Now is the time to recognize which activities are duds and replace them with more engaging ones.

Practice sessions are also helpful in logistical ways. The props crew better understands what to bring out and when. You can see whether chairs and tables are needed. You get a feel for how long each activity will take, and whether you need to have an extra activity or two ready in the wings to fill any vacant time spaces. Team coaches also see more clearly how each activity operates, so they will be able to facilitate play better for their teams.

The themed special events outlined in Section 2 were effective and enjoyable for the many groups I have had the privilege of leading. As you practice the activities, consider the interests, ages, and abilities of your group. Modify the activities appropriately and in a safe manner to accommodate your players.

Organizing the Props

Most of the activities you lead will need props of some sort. I have found an easy way to keep the props organized and your props crew sane. Give each member of your props crew a "cheat sheet" that outlines the order of activities for the event. For each activity, list who is leading it, what props are needed, and a brief description of how the activity is conducted. Assemble the props needed for each activity, and place them in a paper bag with the activity name written on the side in large letters. Set each activity's bag on a table or on the floor in the order in which the activities will be conducted. During your event, the props crew can follow along on their sheet, presenting and removing props efficiently. By using this approach, your props crew feels like they have what they need, they know what needs to be done, and they know when to do it. They succeed, the program flows very smoothly, and everyone is happier.

Final Run-Through

Once you and the leadership team have determined which activities will be presented during your themed special event, and have gathered the necessary props and helpers, it's time for the final run-through. A dress rehearsal of sorts, this final practice session allows you to iron out any wrinkles that might remain in the event. It also gives all your assistants an opportunity to refine their roles. Hand the props crew all the supplies they will need for the program, and their "cheat sheet" of which games need which props. Allow the Scorekeeper, Candy Meister, and Announcer to figure out the particulars of their respective jobs. As you run through each activity, let your assistants execute their roles as they will the night of your event. This final run-through is an effective way to assure you are truly ready for "Show Time!"

Creating a Welcoming Environment

Everyone likes to feel valued. One way you can do this is by creating a welcoming environment for your themed special event. A number of factors combine to make this happen.

Anticipate some of the potential thoughts and feelings your participants may have so you can be sure to create a welcoming environment. Pretend you are a participant arriving at your event's venue for the first time. Am I sure I am in the right place? Will I know where to park and where to enter the building? Once inside, where do I go? Should I really be here—do they really want *me* to be here? Now that I am here, what do I do to not feel awkward? What if I don't know anyone?

Signage that welcomes your guests as they enter the property or facility is a simple touch that can make a big difference in reassuring each person they are in the right place and you are expecting them.

Assign some competent and personable team members to work the registration table. These Greeters will be your first contacts with participants. Make sure they understand the critically important role they play in making your guests feel welcome and at home. Choose people with outgoing personalities and infectious smiles for this role. Give them the materials and information they need to answer questions and to engage each person as soon as he or she arrives. If your participants have registered in advance, prepare nametags for them. They'll be delighted to see you were expecting them!

Once each guest has registered and received a nametag, personally invite them to try out one of the Group Starter activities. This will get them into the theme right away. Give them something constructive to do; this will chase away any last minute thoughts they might have of sneaking out the back door and going home. Instruct each member of your leadership team to personally welcome every person as they arrive and initiate conversation. Each leadership team member may not actually greet every single person. But if they all know they share that responsibility, no guest should be overlooked. Personal contact makes a positive impact on our guests. That is what we want our programs to do, and the moment they walk into our site is the time to begin.

Chapter 4

Tips for a
Smooth Running Event

Whipped cream on pumpkin pie. Sprinkles on your cookies. A friendly smile at the end of a hard day. Sometimes it's the little things that make the biggest differences. In this chapter we'll look at some of those "little things" that go a long way in making your event successful and enjoyable for all.

Preparation

Preparation is the key to a successful event. In previous chapters we reviewed the importance of practicing your activities, sharing information with your leadership team, and having props and other supplies ready to go. All these things combine to help you to be prepared for your themed special event. Adequate preparation contributes greatly to the confidence your leadership team will feel as they welcome your guests to this event. They will know everything is gathered and ready to go. They will be well-acquainted with the schedule for the event, as well as with their individual roles. Preparation and practice set up your event and your leaders for success!

Group Management and Smooth Transitions Between Activities

Any time you have more participants than leaders present, you've got a need for group management. Managing your group does not mean preventing them from having fun. What it does mean is keeping the entire group focused on the activities at hand.

Group management begins even before your participants arrive. As you plan the order of your activities, consider the Programming

Wave. (See my first book, *The Game Finder,* for more information about the Programming Wave.) Begin the main event with the entire group together. Welcome everyone and introduce your theme and your leadership team. Select a creative way for dividing into teams, if you will be using them. If moving participants into teams is a "game," no one will have time to whine about who they are with (or without) on their team. They are into teams and onto the next game before they realize what has happened. Consider the format of each activity you will be leading. Sequence activities that require relay lines back to back in the order of events, and schedule circle games (in which chairs and participants are in a circle formation) one after another. The fewer times you change how people are arranged, the fewer chances you have of losing people in the transition.

How you transition between activities can also maintain group control. An alert and well-rehearsed props crew will keep activities flowing quickly and smoothly, which keeps the group's attention focused on the leader. If you anticipate the transition to take extra time due to clean up or set up requirements, consider adding a filler activity. Notice quiz questions are included in the Banana-Rama and Chocola-Mania events. Rounds of these theme-related trivia questions between activities keep the participants focused on your program, not on making mischief or losing interest.

During your program, there are several effective techniques for maintaining group control. First of all, have theme-related Group Starters available for participants to enjoy while they wait for the formal program to begin. Idle hands and minds tend to find something to do; let's be sure to provide constructive options.

Train your staff to interact with your participants, especially those who seem to be uninvolved or negatively involved. As your leadership team reaches out and draws in your guests, they are establishing a rapport that will be maintained throughout the program. This is positive group management.

When it is time to begin the formal part of your themed special event, take time to introduce the program and the leaders. If the group is not too big, let them introduce themselves as well. Set a tone for positive interactions and involvement at the beginning.

As you and your Leadership Team conduct activities, make sure you have plenty of assistants not actively involved in leading the game. Each team should have at least one Team Coach, who is responsible for maintaining order in his or her team. If you know your group has the potential to be "distracted" easily, you may want to start off with two Team Coaches per team. If possible, have a floater or two assigned just to keep a lookout for situations which may require additional adult intervention. Empower them to award bonus points to teams who are attentive and well-behaved. Remember: rewarded behaviors tend to be repeated.

The goal with these group management techniques is to keep the participants focused on the event you have planned. By doing so, participants who tend to create their own excitement due to boredom or need for attention will have their attention focused on the fun at hand. If our programs are exciting and well-prepared, we should be able to avoid most potential problems.

Music

Music! The universal language has the power to soothe the savage beast, and the ability to create an incredible atmosphere for your themed special event. When I present creative programming workshops, I love to do an exercise that illustrates the power music has for transforming an ordinary activity into a magical montage of motion. Try this for yourself. Give a foam wand to each of two people, and ask them to whack each other gently with them. Observe for a minute, then turn on the theme from *Star Wars*. What a transformation in the level of excitement and involvement you will see! Magically, Luke Skywalker and Darth Vader appear right before your very eyes. No longer are your two volunteers ordinary people. They have been transformed into Jedi Knights who are larger than life. That kind of transformation is what brings excitement to lives, and participants to your events.

Use appropriate background music to establish the atmosphere you want as your guests arrive. Select some lively tunes to play during your active games. As you cool down your program, fill the air with more soothing, theme-related music. When your participants hear these songs again, they may well recall the fun they had and the positive feelings they felt as a result of having attended your themed special event.

Chapter 5

Making Our Guests Feel Special

When we head home to Pennsylvania for Thanksgiving, we know Grandma and Pap have been anticipating our arrival: the kitchen counter is laden with pumpkin pies—my husband's favorite food! Sure, it's a traditional dish for this holiday, but Grandma always makes sure they are baked before we get there, so we know she's been anticipating our visit. While you don't necessarily need to bake pies, you should make it obvious you are looking forward to having your participants join you for this occasion. In this chapter, we'll look at ways to make our guests feel special at our events.

Personal Welcome

Perhaps the first and most obvious gesture is to greet each guest with a smile and a personal welcome. These simple acts go far in assuring a timid visitor his or her presence is appreciated and he or she is a special member of the group. I believe the tone you set in this initial contact greatly influences the positive impact your program will have on each person. First impressions are vital to your program's success. Make sure you give all people the right first impression—they are valued and in for a great experience.

The Magic of a Name

The sweetest sound to people's ears is to hear someone call their name. Our name is our identity. It's personal. Calling someone by his or her name communicates, "I know you, and I care about you."

As your guests arrive, welcome them by name if possible. Assist them in getting signed in. If your participants registered in advance, have a nametag ready for them. This does two important things. First, it lets the participant know you've been expecting them to join you. Second, it allows you to print their name in large, easy to read block letters. With each person donning an easily read nametag, leaders can greet each person by name. People love to hear someone call them by name, to speak to them personally. When you register your partici- pants, be sure to ask them how they would like their name to appear on their nametags. Some people may prefer a more formal name; oth- ers may prefer a nickname. What is important is for our participants to feel comfortable and for us to call them by the name they prefer.

As you are conducting the program, these nametags will be very helpful and will make for a more personal event. Since everyone will have a legible nametag on, the leader can say, "Everyone from Bob to Susan will be one group," instead of saying, "Everyone between the guy in the red shirt and the woman in the striped blouse are togeth- er." Not only will Bob and Susan feel special, but everyone else now knows Bob and Susan, too. These personal touches distinguish a good program from a very special one.

Group Welcome

Another opportunity for a "personal touch" for your program is dur- ing the group welcome. At the beginning of your program, once the group has arrived, take a few minutes to formally introduce your pro- gram and the leadership team. Use a simple statement like, "Welcome to [name of your themed special event]. We're glad you could join us this evening! My name is Annette Moore, and I will be your MC for the evening. Also on the leadership team are..." If your group is not too large, you may want to pass around a theme-related prop, and let each participant share their name with the group when the prop is passed to them. Either way, do take time to officially welcome your group and thereby signal the beginning of the event.

Smiles, Eye Contact, and Atta Boys

Throughout the event, take advantage of opportunities to smile at and make eye contact with your participants and your leadership team. Both will benefit from these brief yet personal affirmations. Be liberal with your praise and encouragement, even if a team loses a relay or activity. Our objective is to build up and to encourage all those involved. Remember, regardless of their team's scores, each person is a winner, a valuable asset to the group, and a vital contributor to the success of the event. Your actions should communicate that.

A Personal Thank You

At the end of your program, you have another wonderful opportunity to affirm and to acknowledge each person who contributed to the successful event—everyone! Just as you formally welcomed the group to initiate the event, formally conclude the program. Not only does this give the participants the clear message that they are now dismissed, but also it gives you a chance to thank them for attending and to thank your leadership team for their hard work. It also gives the participants the opportunity to collectively applaud and thank you and your team for a delightful event. As your participants exit, work with your leadership team to personally thank each person for attending—and invite them back for your next gathering! Beyond the individual benefits, these simple personal touches go far in developing positive public relations between your agency and your clientele.

Documenting the Fun

Continue to make your participants feel special even after the event by documenting the fun they had. Photos taken during the event can be displayed on a bulletin board, on a website, or in an agency newsletter.

These visuals remind participants of the enjoyable experience they had together with you and may stimulate others to join in the fun next time. Pictures, videos, props, and images make lasting memories—not only of the activities themselves, but also of the joyful feelings associated with your event, with the people, and with your agency. Consider recruiting a volunteer "Memory Maker" to document and display these fun reminders of your themed special event.

Chapter 6

Making Your Leadership Team Feel Special

A coach may be famous and talented, but the players actually play and win the game. It is much the same with leading themed special events. You may be very gifted and even well-known as a program planner. But it is the whole leadership team working together that creates and implements a successful program. It takes each member of the leadership team to reach the participants who join you for an event. As one person, you can't be everywhere, see everything, or talk to every person. You need each member of the leadership team, working in harmony, to accomplish this feat. You need their complementary skills and personalities to develop each aspect of the event. If you were successful, if the event was successful, it was because of the combined efforts of the leadership team. Let's look at ways to honor your team.

Delegating Responsibility

Everyone likes to feel important. You can help your leadership team members feel important by having each one be responsible for some of the component tasks of the event. Divide the program into discrete tasks. Determine the talents and skills of each team member, and delegate tasks to the appropriate people. This "matching talent with task" step is a key to successful delegation. I had a team member tell me once, "I'll help out with anything but decorations. I don't do frilly stuff." I put her in charge of gathering the prizes. She had a great time, she did a wonderful job, and she knew it!

When we give people responsibilities, they feel challenged and valued. As viable members of the team, they will feel ownership of part of the program and its success. They have the potential to achieve great things by completing their component tasks. Give your team members opportunities to contribute and to succeed: delegate!

Setting Them Up for Success

As the Event Coordinator, you can help your Leadership Team members be successful. If you have delegated planning tasks to them, make sure they have the information and resources they need to complete those tasks. Follow up with them to assure they are making progress and will be ready by the due date, but remember to give them the freedom to do their jobs.

Give Game Leaders opportunities to practice leading their games in front of others. The more they practice, the more proficient they will become—and the more confident. Set your Game Leaders up for success by giving them opportunities to perfect their skills.

If information is power, make your Leadership Team as strong as possible. Any relevant information you have, share with the team. As much as possible, give the information to them in writing, so there is no question about what you mean. Each team member should have a copy of the order of activities for your event. Include the activity's title, leader, props, and brief description. Make sure the Props Crew, Scorekeeper, Announcer, and Candy Meister have copies, too. The better your helpers understand what is going to happen, the more they can help facilitate it. We don't call them a Leadership Team for nothing!

Make Your Leaders Stand Out

Another way to set your Leadership Team up for success is by setting them apart from the participants. Yes, we do want them to mingle with our guests, and to participate in the fun. But we also want the participants to recognize who the leaders are. One way to distinguish the Leadership Team is by having them wear a special shirt. These shirts could be specially designed for your event, or simply select brightly colored shirts for the team to wear. If your event is of a sports theme, a shirt with black and white vertical stripes would be appropriate. If you don't have the funds for staff shirts, let the leaders wear any dark colored shirt, and give them a brightly colored sash to wear. Sashes could be made of strips of fabric, ribbon, or surveyor's tape. If your event will be outdoors, a special hat or visor may be an appropriate addition. While drawing the attention of the participants, Leadership Team members in "uniform" are easily spotted by other team members, plus their "insignia" makes them feel the importance of their roles.

Publicly Recognizing Leaders and Their Efforts

Certainly, you will want to publicly thank your Leadership Team at the conclusion of your event. Since they were critically important to the successful execution of every detail, you will want to let people know how valuable they are. Your delighted participants, too, will want to applaud their efforts in providing such a wonderful experience for them.

Beyond these immediate opportunities to say thank you to your Leadership Team, seek avenues for broader recognition. Include photos of these folks on your bulletin board, in your agency newsletter, and on your website. Write a letter to the editor of your local paper to publicly acknowledge their efforts.

Thank-You Messages

Just as a personal touch was important for affirming your participants, a personal thank-you to each member of your Leadership Team is also important. Beyond the verbal thank-you remarks, give them some tangible message of appreciation. A simple, handwritten thank-you note can be read and reread. If appropriate, drop a note to the worker's boss, letting him or her know what an asset this individual was to your Leadership Team. Who knows, it may help them get a well-deserved raise or promotion during their annual review!

Personally, I like to be creative. After one event, I bought beach balls and wrote on them in permanent marker, "I had a ball working with you on the Beach Party!" One of those key helpers still has that beach ball; I saw her young children playing with it recently! Seasonally, you can purchase those giant Hershey chocolate Kisses. Attach a note that says, "You were so much help at our event, I had to give you a big kiss!" A little creativity can go a long way in making someone feel special.

Themed special events are such fun for participants, and they can be very satisfying and great fun for you, the Event Coordinator, as well. I hope this overview of program planning considerations has given you a good basis on which to build your programs. Now that we've reviewed the foundational blocks for building a successful themed special event, let's move on to the great themed special events themselves!

Section 2

The Plans

Banana-Rama

Bananas: what a versatile fruit. You can toss them, push them, pass them, even eat them! Try out this program on your group. You'll realize there's a lot of fun to be had for only 59¢ a pound!

Atmosphere Enhancers

Create a jungle-like atmosphere by creating banana plants (like palm trees, with wider leaves) out of colored paper and taping them to the walls. Add a few colorful parrots and a golden sun to complete the scene. Ask your local grocer to save a few empty banana crates for you to set out as well.

Arrange chairs to form a polygon with as many sides as you will have teams. Depending on how many participants you expect, you may need for each side (team) to have two rows of chairs.

Ask participants to bring two bananas each, and to come dressed in as much yellow as possible. Outlandish is helpful for setting a tone of fruity frivolity!

Getting Ready

Set up a registration table near the entrance to your game area. Have teams already divided, or have roster sheets prepared for guests to sign up for a team. If you are expecting the crowd to be of mixed ages or abilities, prepare sign-up sheets for each team with slots for Adults, Big Kids (ages 9 to 12), and Little Kids (ages 5 to 8).

- Have nametags ready for each participant, plus extras, and markers.

- Color code nametags to distinguish teams.

- Arrange a table for the Guess the Number of Chips contest. Count the number of banana chips you place in a glass jar. Set out a pen and tablet of paper.

- Cover a large table or two with paper or a vinyl tablecloth. Set out markers (fine tip), pens, felt fabric and paper scraps, tape, toothpicks, and aluminum foil. Create a "Bananimal" so guests get an idea of what they are to do.

- Set aside at least 16 bananas of equal size per team. Some of these will be used for eating events, so pick "nice" ones. Wash them.

- Line playing area with chairs, enough so each participant will have a chair. Chairs should be arranged in a square or polygon, so each row of chairs will hold one team. Ideal team size is 12–16 players.

- Color code each team's row of chairs for ease in locating the correct place to sit.

- Locate several banquet style tables, allowing for one table for every two teams.

- Ready a large plastic tarp or sheet for placing under the bins for Banana Bobbing.

- Locate plastic storage bins of equal size, one per team, for Banana Bobbing. Clean the insides, and fill one half to three quarters full with water. (Be sure to get help lifting these bins—water is heavy!)

- Find a large garbage can, empty it, and put a clean trash can liner in it. Set aside for Bananas in Space.

- Create 15-inch to 18-inch bananas out of sturdy, yellow paper for the "Musical Bananas" game. Allow for two "bananas" per team.

- Set up CD player with some calypso music to play during Musical Bananas.

- Secure for each team: a bandana, straw hat, banana and a warm (room temperature) 12-ounce can of 7-Up for the Shoot Out.

- Have the "Know Your Banana" question and answer sheet ready.

- Recruit someone to act as official Scorekeeper.

- Create a scoreboard with columns for each team and rows for each game. Keep score as events happen.

- Secure banana-related prizes for winners of Guess the Number of Chips, Banana Bob, Musical Bananas, Shoot Out at the Chiquita Corral, and Couple's Banana Feed. For example, the Banana Chip jar could be given to the person who guesses closest to the actual number.

- Prepare banana ribbons or awards for winners from various categories for Best Bananimal (e.g., prettiest, most creative, most animal-like, most bizarre).

- Have a supply of paper towels on hand—just in case things get messy!

- Set up refreshment table.

Group Starters

Guess the Number of Chips

As participants arrive, have them make a guess of how many banana chips are in the jar, and write the number next to their name on a sheet of paper set by the jar. After everyone has made a guess, have an assistant determine a winner, based on the actual number of banana chips in the jar.

Bananimals

Invite guests to create a "bananimal" out of a banana and the miscellaneous items you have assembled at a crafts table. (Encourage creativity!) Use items such as markers, pens, felt, fabric and paper scraps,

tape, toothpicks, and aluminum foil to transform a banana into a stupendous creation.

Welcome and Introductions

Ask guests to sit in their teams, according to the color coding of their nametags. Make sure each team's row of chairs is clearly marked to facilitate this process.

Welcome to Banana-Rama! After this evening's festivities, you will never look at a banana in quite the same way! Of course, that's assuming you ever want to look at another banana after tonight! We're going to have a lot of fun with bananas of all sorts. Let's get our program started by familiarizing ourselves with this humble, yet lovable, fruit.

Team Events

Banana Pass

Leaders hand a banana to the person from each team who is sitting in the right-most chair. On the "go" command, have teams pass the banana person to person by hand, from the first player to the last, and back again. Ask the person who was first to move to the last position, and have everyone else slide up a chair. Also do this after each event, to allow more people the opportunity to be first.

Have the teams repeat the above procedure, this time conveying the banana by holding it between feet, passing it to next person without allowing it to fall to the floor. Award Banana Chips (aka, points) to the winning teams.

Banana Jam Relay

Place a stack of banana boxes in the center of your playing area. Hand the right-most player from each team a banana. This time, the people holding the bananas race to the center of the playing area, run counterclockwise around the stack of boxes (left shoulders should be on the box side), and take a seat at the end of their team's row. This seat should now be vacant, as the rest of the team should have shifted one seat to the right while the banana holder was running. The banana is passed person-to-person back to the new right-most player. Once she receives the banana, this player takes off, racing around the center obstacle in a counterclockwise direction, and returning to the left end, empty chair. The race continues until each team has returned their first player (and what's left of the well-squeezed banana!) to the right-most position.

Leaders: Have one or two people on the Leadership Team stand in the center of the playing area to direct traffic (to minimize traffic jams and collisions). Players tend to concentrate more on speed than on which side of the box they are on!

Know Your Banana

Game show style, a leader asks teams various banana-related questions. Players try to correctly answer the banana trivia quiz questions, and win "Banana Chips" for their team.

Note: Use "Know Your Banana" between events that require a lot of set up. This will keep participants involved and minimize down time. Therefore, don't ask all the questions at this point in the evening!

Bananas in Space

Each team competes separately and in turn for this event. Give a banana to each person on the first team. From their seats, players toss their bananas into a box that is placed in the center of the playing area. Place a vinyl cloth under the box. After the first team has tossed all their bananas, tally number of bananas in the box, remove them, and proceed with the next team.

Banana Bobbing

While the set-up crew removes the box and bananas from the last game, replace them with tubs of water, and get one volunteer to compete for each team. This event is a speed race. Team representatives will get 60 seconds to remove as many bananas from the tubs of water as possible—using their

mouths only! Place a dozen bananas in each of the tubs. Have participants kneel on the floor in front of their tub, and begin timing! At the end of 60 seconds, count and see which person removed the most bananas.

Leaders: Assign an assistant to each player. If the participant successfully removes all 12 bananas and time remains, put some of them back into the tub, so the player may continue. Just remember that you did so, so an accurate count may be made.

Musical Bananas

Select four representatives per team. Place banana shaped papers on the floor. While appropriate calypso music plays, participants walk along circle. When the music stops, participants race to stand on a banana. Players (and bananas) are eliminated until only one of each remains.

Partners Banana Feed

Each team selects a couple to represent them. Banquet tables should be set up in the center of the playing area, so partners stand across the table from each other. Set a banana on the table between each couple. (Allow space for two to three couples per table, depending on the length of the table.) On the "go" signal, each couple races to see who can pick up, peel, and consume their banana first without using hands! Have plenty of paper towels on hand for the conclusion of this event!

Shoot Out at the Chiquita Corral

Recruit one competitor per team. Give each chosen player a neck bandana, a cowboy hat, a banana, and a 12-ounce can of warm 7-Up. Have players start in the center of the playing area, back to back, with bananas and sodas in hand. In unison, have players step off five paces. On the "go" signal, players compete to see who can consume their banana and entire can of soda first. (This will become quite frothy: have paper towels ready!)

Cool Down and Refreshments

Finish asking "Know Your Banana" quiz questions and award prizes (something "banana-y") for

- best bananimal (e.g., prettiest, most creative, most animal-like, most bizarre).

- guess the number of banana chips.

- the team with the most banana chip points.

Special thank-you's to participants and to members of the leadership team for a super slimy, stupendous event! Invite everyone to partake of the banana refreshments:

- banana bread, banana muffins, banana cookies, bananas.

- banana splits.

- banana fondue (dip banana chunks into warmed hot fudge sauce).

Questions for "Know Your Banana"

1. Banana plants are which of the following?
   A. Perennials
   B. **Annuals**

2. Bananas are native to the East Indies and were later introduced to Central America.
   A. **True**
   B. False

3. Individual bananas grow in large clumps called
   A. Flocks
   B. Herds
   C. **Bunches**

4. About how many bunches of bananas are imported to the United States every year?
   A. 5
   B. **75 million**
   C. 4.2 zillion

5. Bananas are sold in stores in clusters called a
   A. **Hand**
   B. Foot
   C. Cerebral cortex

6. The banana belongs to the genus
   A. Bananacus
   B. **Musa**
   C. Dairy Queenus Splittius

7. What color are banana flowers?
   A. Green
   B. **Yellow**
   C. Pink
   D. Hunter's "blaze orange"

8. How many buds does a banana plant produce?
   A. **One**
   B. 30 to 50
   C. Over 100

9. Banana plants are usually about 10 to 20 feet tall.
    A. **True**
    B. False

10. The stalk of the banana plant is not wood. It is made up of the bases of leaves.
    A. **True**
    B. False

11. How many clusters of bananas are there in an average bunch?
    A. 5
    B. **6 to 15**
    C. 20 to 30

12. An individual banana is called a
    A. Fruit
    B. **Finger**
    C. Toe
    D. Yellow Thingie-Doodle

13. The banana fruit is over 75% water.
    A. **True**
    B. False

14. The plantain is a type of banana that needs to be cooked before eaten.
    A. **True**
    B. False

15. Bananas can be eaten raw, baked, fried, or drunk as banana beer.
    A. **True**
    B. False

16. Banana plants are also used to make which of the following?
    A. Paper
    B. Twine
    C. Wrapping material
    D. **All of the above**

17. The banana plant is a(n)
    A. Tree
    B. **Herb**
    C. Overused joke

18. On the plant, the individual bananas
    A. Droop downward
    B. **Point upward**
    C. Spiral in all directions
    D. Change orientations with the cycles of the moon

19. There are usually over 200 individual bananas in a bunch.
    A. True
    B. **False (there are actually 50 to 150)**

20. Each banana plant produces how many bunches before it is cut
    down?
    A. **One**
    B. Two
    C. 5 to 10
    D. Many zillion

21. One of Elvis Presley's favorite foods was a fried peanut butter and
    banana sandwich.
    A. **True**
    B. False

22. In which of the following colors do bananas not occur?
    A. Yellow
    B. Red
    C. **Purple**

23. The underground stem of the banana plant lives for many years
    and produces many banana plants.
    A. **True**
    B. False

24. The United State imports more bananas than any other country.
    A. **True**
    B. False

25. Bananas are frequently ripened artificially after shipping using ethylene gas.
   A. **True**
   B. False

26. Bananas are shipped in specially designed refrigerated ships.
   A. **True**
   B. False

27. Bananas are high in carbohydrates.
   A. **True**
   B. False

28. There are more than 300 varieties of bananas.
   A. **True**
   B. False

29. Banana plants are grown from
   A. Seeds
   B. **Cuttings from other banana plants**
   C. Discarded banana split bowls

30. "Banana" most closely rhymes with
   A. **Bandana**
   B. Metaphysics
   C. Recreation Leader

31. How many seeds are there in the average banana?
   A. None
   B. 4 to 6
   C. **More than you can count!**

32. Ripeness of bananas is rated on a seven-point scale. What color is a number one banana?
   A. **Green**
   B. Yellow
   C. Brown

33. Chiquita is a registered trademark of what company?
   A. International Fruit
   B. **United Brands**
   C. Harley Davidson

34. Which of the following countries is not a major banana producer?
    A. Honduras
    B. Ethiopia
    C. **Chad**
    D. Taiwan

35. The first records of the banana are from 500–600 B.C. from
    A. **India**
    B. Africa
    C. Honduras
    D. Asheville, NC

36. The banana was introduced to the "New World" in
    A. **1516**
    B. 1622
    C. 1703
    D. None; it's native here.

37. The name of the company that began the Central American banana trade was
    A. Chiquita
    B. **United Fruit Company**
    C. Central American Banana, Inc.
    D. Mello Yellow

38. The first banana variety brought to England was the
    A. **Dwarf Cavendish**
    B. Gros Michel
    C. Manta Handurias
    D. Brown Slimer

39. M. C. Keith was the "pioneer of the Central American Banana Trade."
    A. **True**
    B. False

40. The first banana steamship was the
    A. Love Boat
    B. S.S. Salvador
    C. **S.S. Bowden**
    D. S.S Plantain

41. Which of the following is not a serious banana pest?
    A. Rust Thrips
    B. Banana Wilt
    C. Scab Moth
    D. Banana Borer
    E. **All are serious banana pests**

42. Bunchy Top disease is a serious threat to banana production.
    A. **True**
    B. False

43. Which banana variety is generally considered to have the best bunch form, color, and texture?
    A. **Gros Michel**
    B. Lacatan
    C. Dwarf Cavendish
    D. Jonathan Wimberus

44. Banana beer is popular in East Africa.
    A. **True**
    B. False

Beach Party

Winter dragging on? Here's an idea for beating the winter doldrums: a beach party! Creating a beach-like environment really draws the crowd into the program. Set up lots of beach chairs and umbrellas, and lay out colorful beach towels, sand buckets, and beach balls. Suspend a brightly colored kite, crank up the Beach Boys tunes, and smear on some cocoa butter. Looks, sounds, and smells like summer to me!

Setting

- Crank up the heat!

- Decorate area with beach paraphernalia (e.g., beach chairs, umbrellas, towels, sand buckets, shovels, beach balls, kites).

- If possible, set up a sandbox with castle-making implements.

- Set up CD player with Beach Boys music playing in the background.

Getting Ready

- Set up registration table.

- Nametags for participants at registration table should be color-coded in advance to distinguish teams. Plan to have at least four teams of 8–12 players. Add more teams as needed to maintain the optimal number per team.

- Have color-coded construction paper taped to floor where teams will line up. These colors should correspond to the teams' colors.

- Tape another color-coded piece of construction paper on the wall in front of where each team will stand.

- Inflate beach balls (one per team) and place in a large plastic bag. Have at least one extra available, in case one is defective.

- Prepare a blank 5 x 5 grid Beach Bingo card for each player (use cardstock to make the card sturdier). Also have a pencil ready for each player.

- Acquire several sand buckets for collecting the used bingo cards and pencils.

- Prepare posterboard with "Beach Bingo" written on top and have markers available for keeping track of items called out by the leader.

- Have a pencil and note card for the leader to use to jot down unusual items people are marking on cards for Beach Bingo.

- Have enough decks of playing cards for each person to have one card.

- List the "poker" hands you want to assemble for Deal the Deck.

- Assign leaders to each assist with a different team. Assign someone to ready props for the next game while you lead the current one.

- Prepare posterboard for keeping track of team scores. List each team across the top. Decorate the sign with appropriate beach symbols.

- Recruit someone to be the Scorekeeper. This will be a full-time job for someone once the games get started. The scorekeeper will write the appropriate number of points earned from each game for each team. Award 1,000 points for first place, 900 for second place, 800 points for third place. All other teams get 500 points for participating.

- Mark end line, approximately 40 feet in front of each team's starting line.

- Put zinc oxide in small paper cups, two cups per team.

- Locate folding beach chairs or folding chairs (one per team). Place a beach towel and pair of sunglasses on each.

- Ready one bag or bowl of baked-style potato chips for each team. Set out of reach and out of sight, or they will get eaten ahead of time!

- Divide paper bag stack into groups of as many players as will be on each team. Have a few extras ready for mishaps.

- Theme from Hawaii Five-O cued up.

- Ready one "canoe" for each team. Duct tape three copy paper boxes together to form a long canoe of three chambers. Make sure they are securely fastened.

Prizes Needed

- Candy or small treat, like a plastic lei, for those who came in costume.

- Beach Bingo winner. You may want to have two or three of these, in case more than one person has bingo. You may also chose to continue calling items even after the first person has won, to allow for more winners (and more prizes).

- Team prizes—something simple that commemorates a job well-done for the winning team

Refreshments

Have the "Snack Shack" set up with treats such as popsicles, Italian ices or snow cones, salt-water taffy, chips, or popcorn

Proper Attire

Leadership team should dress in beach or Hawaiian styles: Shorts, Hawaiian shirts, sandals, sun hat, shades. Encourage participants to come in summer play clothes (but not bathing suits). Award small prizes to all those who come in proper attire.

Welcome and Introductions

It is always great to hit the beach. And when the temperature outside is below freezing, we're really happy to escape to warm, sunny beaches! Thanks for joining us today in this tropical paradise. Surf's up—let's dive into some fun.

Icebreakers and Mixers

Beach Bingo

Each person receives a bingo card and a pencil, and writes her name in the center (free) square. On "go," everyone mingles around, asking others to write something they would take to the beach. Each person may fill in only one square on any other person's bingo card. After five minutes of mingling and filling in blank squares, the group reconvenes. The leaders call out items one-by-one by, and participants "X" out squares with matching items. When a participant has five in a row, he or she yells "bingo!" The items are checked, and the person wins a prize. Leaders: You may choose to continue calling items, thus allowing a few more people to win bingo.

> **Leaders:** During these five minutes, you mingle around as well, and observe what people are writing. Include some of the unusual ones (like Spam) along with the "normal" items you might expect (e.g., towel, sunscreen, beach chair).

> **Assistants:** After the bingo prize is awarded, collect bingo cards and pencils in beach buckets and set them aside.

Author's note: Playing cards in the evening is an important family tradition when we go to beach. We usually play Hearts, but then we don't usually have this big of a crowd!

Deal the Deck

Distribute playing cards to your participants, one per person. Leader calls out a poker-type hand (four of a kind, two pair, full house, flush), and participants scramble to get into those groups. You may add variations. For example declare face cards 10 points, other cards as face value, and then have folks gather in groups of five to total 30 points.

Team Dividing

Divide group into teams, and have them line up single file behind construction paper of their color. (Nametags should be color coded ahead of time.) Have team captains/leaders count how many players their team has, and adjust teams as necessary to equalize numbers.

Team Relays/Games

If you need a little extra time preparing for the next relay, call for a dance break—turn on a tune, and let everyone dance (in place) until the next event is ready to go.

Beach Ball Pass (With Variations)

Give each team an inflated beach ball. Have them pass the ball person to person, beginning at the front of the line. When the last person gets the beach ball, he runs to the front of the line and starts the ball pass again. Play ends when the original starting person is in his original position, holding the beach ball, and the team is seated on the floor.

- Pass between legs. Same game, with different mode of passing.

- Over and under. Players pass the ball again, with each player alternately passing it over one's head or between one's legs.

Partner Pairs

Teammates get a partner, and line up by twos. A beach ball is placed between the two players. While holding the ball between them, they must run up to the end line (approximately 40 feet away) and back, then place the beach ball between the next couple.

Partner Protection

Nobody wants a sunburned nose! Partners hold hands and run to end line. A team leader is waiting there, holding two cups with zinc oxide in them. One partner covers his eyes with his hands while the other partner takes a small amount of zinc oxide on her finger, spins around five times, and applies the zinc oxide to her partner's nose. Roles reverse, the cups with zinc oxide in them remain with the team leader, and the partners race back to tag off the next pair.

I Love the Sun

Now that we're all "properly protected," we can really enjoy the sun! Each team gets a folding chair, a beach towel, and a pair of shades. In turn, each player runs up to the end line, sets up the chair, throws the towel around his or her shoulders, sticks on the shades, sits back in the chair, and yells "I LOVE THE SUN!" Then he or she stands up, removes the shades and towel, folds up the chair, and races back to the team, handing off the beach props to the next person in line.

The Lay's Challenge

Eat just one potato chip! Team members take turns running up to the end line, taking one potato chip from the team's bowl, chewing and swallowing it completely (to the Judge's satisfaction), then racing back to touch off the next player.

> **Note:** Please use baked potato chips. Regular fried potato chips are too sharp and not as safe to use in this game.

> **Leaders:** Each Team Coach needs a bowl of baked potato chips (e.g., Baked Lays), with enough chips for each player to have at least one chip. (You'll also need a strong stomach, since you'll be checking each player's mouth for chips!)

Author's note: Playing football on the beach is a real blast. Good fun. Good exercise. Good opportunity to really "strut your stuff " when you score.

"We Bad" Relay

Each player gets a paper lunch bag. On the "go" signal, players take turns running up to the end line, blowing up the bag, popping it, spiking it down, and doing a five-second "victory dance." When the Team Coach says five seconds is up, that player races back to the team and tags off the next player.

Hawaii Five-0

With theme song playing in the background, three team members at a time stand close together with one foot in their cardboard "canoe." Players "paddle" with their arms while propelling with their legs to end point, approximately 10 yards away. Once there, the threesome leaves their canoe, races back to the team and tags off the next trio, who run "across the beach" to the canoe, and paddle it back. Song is approximately two minutes and 15 seconds long. Depending on the number of canoeing trios, you may need to replay the theme song.

Cool Down

The Wave

You know what is the best part about swimming at the beach: Waves! Lead the group in a quick series of "The Wave"—you know, like at football games. Have teams lined up shoulder to shoulder. Starting at the front of the line, send a wave down and back, then have the team yell, "We love the beach!" Let each team have a turn. Have the first team start a wave again. This time, have the second team begin as soon as the first team finishes, so each team becomes part of a continual wave. Have the teams circle up to allow for one continual wave—a tsunami!

Whirlpool

To the music "Wipe Out," all join hands, making a long line, with the leader at the front of the line. Run around room, spiraling into the center and out again. End with the group in a large circle for thank-yous.

> **Leaders:** Be sure you are only jogging slowly, taking small steps. The "tail" of your line will experience great "whiplash" if you run too quickly.

Award Team Prizes

While you are leading The Wave and Whirlpool, have your Score-keeper total each team's scores, and order them. Announce each team and its score, beginning with the team with the fewest points. (Even if a team didn't place in any of the games, it should still have 4,500 points. That's respectable!) Finally, announce the team with the most points, and award them a fabulous prize—perhaps a token for a free ice cream cone or a bag of salt-water taffy.

Thank You. Good Night!

Chocola-Mania

News Flash! The Food and Drug Administration has just modified their Nutritional Guide Pyramid. The recently revised chart includes a new foundational level: Chocolate! With a Recommended Daily Allowance of 12 to 15 servings (and don't forget between-meal snacks), it's a dietary change we can all live with!

Atmosphere Enhancers

- Decorate the walls in the play area with enlarged duplicates of various chocolate candy wrappers.

- Set up a CD player to provide background music, like The Candy Man, Lollipop, or similar songs.

Getting Ready

- Arrange chairs in a large square in the playing area and assign each side to a team. Assemble enough chairs on each side so each player has a seat on their team's side of the square. Leave plenty of space in the middle for events.

- Prepare registration table with sign-in sheets organized as team sign-up sheets (Guests sign in by writing their names of a team roster. If you are expecting a mixed group, have a section on each roster for adults/teens, for big kids, and another for younger kids. This will assure that each team has an even mix of ages/abilities.)

- Nametags will need to be marked for use in Line 'em up & Spell 'em out! Divide the nametags into as many stacks as you will have teams. (Allow 10–14 per team.) On the top right corner of the nametag, mark a letter from the team's name. For instance, on the Godiva team stack, the first nametag will be marked with a green "G," the second nametag with a green "O," the third with a green "D," and so on. After the team name has been spelled out, start over again at the beginning of the word, so each nametag has a letter on it in the team's color.

This will enable players to more easily locate their teams. If desired, decorate nametags with the team logo: a Hershey's Kiss (brown letters), a Reese's Peanut Butter Cup (orange letters), a Nestle's Crunch Bar (blue letters), or a Godiva candy bar (green letters). Have several medium tipped permanent markers available for writing on the nametags.

- Photocopy Chocola-Anagrams sheet so each team will have one. Have copies at registration table to hand to the first "big kid" to register on each team. Each team will also need a pencil or pen.

- Prepare Guess the Number of Semi-Sweets in the Jar. Have someone count the number of semi-sweet chocolate pieces put into a clear jar. Set up a table for the jar and for a tablet of lined paper and pen, to record the guesses.

- Prepare Chip Toss playing area. Purchase a large package of "cheap" chocolate chip cookies. Cover a gymnastics mat with a sheet, or use an old comforter as the base for the targets. (This will provide a cushioned surface for the tossed cookies.) Cut large semi-sweet chocolate chip-shaped targets out of brown construction paper or foam crafts sheets. Be prepared with cleaning supplies (e.g., broom, dustpan, trash can).

- Purchase a king-size Tootsie Roll to pass around during introductions.

- Place 10 M&M candies in a three-ounce paper cup for each participant.

- Prepare a sheet of posterboard as a scoreboard. Label it with the four team names across the top. You may want to list the numbers 1–10 down the side of the scoreboard, allowing enough space to write the scores, and any other points ("chips") the team may score in addition to game points.

- Recruit someone to be the Scorekeeper.

- Recruit someone to be the MC (Minister of Chocolate) to be responsible for asking the Chocolate Bowl questions.

- Prepare Chocolate Bowl questions for the person who will be asking them to the teams throughout the event. Make sure the correct answers are marked!

- Purchase a chocolate bunny in a box for each team. Buy "cheap" ones, as they will just be passed, not consumed!

- Ready stacks of damp paper towels in plastic containers (e.g., dishpans or plastic shoebox storage containers), so each team has a plastic container with enough damp paper towels for each person to have one, or have a box of disposable wipes on hand.

- Purchase four 8-ounce bags of Hershey's Kisses for Give Me a Kiss Relay, one bag per team.

- Purchase extra bags of Kisses or other chocolates for periodic "chocolate breaks," as desired.

- Have a trash container available for each team to collect wrappers from the candies.

- Cover four 6-foot or 8-foot banquet tables with paper or vinyl tablecloths.

- Purchase four standard or king-sized Hershey's Chocolate Bars for Meet You in the Middle, one per team.

- Have damp and dry paper towels ready for contestants to use after Meet You in the Middle.

- Assemble props for Donut Dangle. (Be sure to test your "system" before event time.) You will need a large tarp to cover the playing area, four sturdy chairs, 16 to 20 yards of half-inch elastic, scissors, 16 to 20 yards of string, minimum of 16 mini chocolate or chocolate iced donuts, and paper towels for contestants for after the event.

- Design the Donut Dangle set up. The four chairs will be the corners of your square playing area, set atop the tarp. Stretch one quarter of the elastic between each pair of chairs, creating an elastic band perimeter. Tie off the elastic at each chair. Suspend four donuts per side using various lengths of string, tied at least two feet apart on each side. (To save time, tie the strings to the elastic earlier, and wait until the set-up of the game during the event to attach the donuts.)

- Locate four large nonbreakable mixing bowls or jumbo mugs for Swiss Hit or Miss, so each team has use of one.

- Purchase/prepare enough chocolate pudding for each of the mugs to have an inch or two in the bottom and to use in the Sundry Search relay.

- Purchase four 1-pound bags of regular size marshmallows, one per team.

- Find 8 aluminum pie pans and at least 25 long, plastic sundae spoons for Sundry Search, assuming you have four teams. Adjust number to match number of teams you have, times two.

- Materials will be needed for the featured activity you select. See activity description for particular materials you will need to create/purchase/prepare.

Group Starters

Guess the Number of Semi-Sweets in the Jar

Be sure to set out a sheet of paper and a pen so participants can record their guesses.

Chip Toss

Lay out a sheet of foam with targets marked on it. Have early arriving guests try to toss cheap chocolate chip cookies onto the bull's eyes.

Chocola-Anagrams

Challenge people to see how many words they can make from the names of the teams.

Mixers

Welcome to Chocola-mania! Have the group (participants and leaders) assemble in a large circle in the center of the playing area.

Tootsie Roll

What better way to find out who is present than by taking roll—especially with a Tootsie Roll! While the group stands in a circle, a king-size tootsie roll is passed from person-to-person, giving each a chance to tell everyone her name and her favorite kind of chocolate candy.

M&M Meetings

Each person is given a small paper cup with 10 M&M's in it. People then mingle around, introducing themselves to one another. Every time you greet some one, you may eat an M&M. "Greet one, eat one."

Line 'em up & Spell 'em out!

This activity divides the group into teams. Instruct participants to look at the top right corners of their nametags. Each should have a single letter printed on it, in one of four colors (or the number of teams you have). On the "go" signal, participants should race to their respective team area (as indicated by color), and line up quickly, so their letters spell out their team name. H – E – R – S – H – E – Y – ' – S, for example. If a team will have more players than letters in the team name, extra players should line up so as to begin spelling the name again. For example, G – O – D – I – V – A – G – O – D – I. The first team to successfully spell their name (s) using all their team players wins big "chips" (aka, points) for their team!

> **Note**: emergency chocolate breaks may need to be taken throughout the competition (to keep our strength up!).

Team Games/Relays

Team Cheer/Chant

Teams are given three minutes to come up with a cheer or chant for their team, which they will perform for the group now, and periodically throughout the evening's competition. Let teams share their cheer with the group. Team cheer may be given after a team is announced as winner for a particular game.

Chocolate Bunny Challenge

Have teams stand in front of their chairs. Run several versions of this passing game. Begin with a simple person-to-person pass, then proceed on to an over/under relay or two. For the final round, remove the chocolate bunny from its packaging and have teams race one more time!

- Have damp paper towels or wipes ready for contestants to use. This game will get gooey!

- Scorekeeper, award points: 1st round: No "chips" awarded. This was a "dry run." 2nd round: 500 chips for the winning team, 400 chips for second place, 300 chips for 3rd, and 200 chips awarded for the 4th place team.

- Challenging Bare Bunny round involves removing the wrapper: Double the chips!

Hugs and Kisses Relay

Four leader assistants stand in the center of the playing area, each with bag of Hershey's Kisses. Teams sit in their seats. Beginning with the person sitting in the rightmost seat on each team, each player runs up, yells, "Give me a Kiss!" If the judge determines the contestant was not loud enough, the leader yells, "WHAT?" so player has to repeat herself. Once the player has successfully asked for and receives a Kiss, she races back to her team, and hugs the next player in line, sending him on his way to the center for a Kiss. Once back in her seat, the first player eats her Hershey's Kiss! (This way, players aren't running with food in their mouths.)

When the last player gets his or her Kiss, he or she hugs the first person in line, sits down at the back of the line, and the team yells out its name, signifying they have completed the event.

Chocolate Quiz

While members of the leadership team lay out a large plastic tarp in the center of the playing area, and set out four covered tables (parallel to the teams) for the next event, allow the MC (Minister of Chocolate) to ask several Chocolate Quiz questions. Direct one question at a time to each of the teams in a rotating manner. Award 200 bonus chips for each correct answer. (This may also be a good time for a much needed chocolate break! Distribute Kisses to all interested parties.)

M&M Maneuvers

At the right end of each table, place a bowl of M&M's. On the left end of each table, place an empty bowl and a stack of individually wrapped drinking straws. Set a trashcan under the left end of each table.

In this relay, the first player sitting in the rightmost chair is given a straw, and races up to his team's table. Inhaling deeply to create enough suction to lift an M&M from the bowl on the right end of the table, the player transports the candy to the bowl at the left end of the table. After transferring two M&M's across the table, the player deposits his straw in the trashcan, grabs a wrapped straw for the next player and returns to his team, sitting in the vacant, leftmost chair. (While this player was maneuvering M&M's, the rest of his team all shifted one chair to the right, leaving the vacant seat now at the end of the row.) When the first player sits in the vacant chair, he hands the wrapped straw to the person next to him, who continues its person-to-person progress to the new rightmost player. Once she receives the straw, she races up to the table, unwrapping the paper, and begins the M&M maneuvers. Races continue until each player has had a turn and is seated in his original chair.

Have the scorekeeper award 1000, 800, 600, 400 chips for first, second, third, and fourth place teams, respectively.

Meet You in the Middle

This is a couple's eating event. Each team should select an adult or teen couple to represent them.

Contestants stand across from their partners at the tables in the center of the playing area. Place a wrapped, regular-sized Hershey's Chocolate Bar on the table between each couple. On the "go" signal, couples must unwrap and eat their way through the Hershey's candy bar—without using their hands!

Play continues until each team has finished eating their chocolate.

Chocolate Quiz

Leadership team removes tables and sets up for the next event. Set four sturdy chairs just inside the four corners of the tarp. Between each pair of chairs, stretch half-inch elastic. From each of these strands of elastic, tie on four lengths of string, evenly spaced, to allow for four contestants per side. Have someone with clean hands tie a small chocolate (or chocolate iced) donut to the end of each strand, so the donut is approximately 12 inches off the ground. Have an adult sit on each of the chairs, to keep them stable and to watch contestants for signs of choking.

Donut Dangle

Each team puts forward four contestants—two big kids and two littler players. Have contestants lay on the tarp under a donut, so each side of the square has one team representative per side, and so two of the sides have the bigger contestants, and two of the sides have the smaller ones.

On the "go" signal, each person must eat his donut completely, then stand up and shout out his team's name. Each side is scored independently of the others. Award 400 chips for each first place contestant, 300 for each second place, 200 for third, and 100 chips for fourth.

Chocolate Quiz

While the MC is conducting more of the Chocolate Quiz, remove the props from the last activity, leaving the tarp in the center of the playing area. Midway to the center of the tarp, on each side, place a large, nonbreakable mixing bowl or jumbo mug. Each "mug" should have an inch or two of chocolate pudding in the bottom, representing hot cocoa. Have a bag of marshmallows on hand for each team.

Swiss Hit or Miss

Each team is given bag of large-size marshmal-lows, which are distributed among the team members. (A 1-pound bag will have approximate-ly 64 marshmallows in it.) On the "go" signal, all participants throw their marshmallows at their team's bowl of "cocoa," trying to get as many in as possible. Allow 45 to 60 seconds for players to toss the marshmallows.

Have two leaders take the bowls aside and count marshmallows, keeping track of which be-longed to which team.

Award 100 chips for each marshmallow in the team's "cocoa mug."

Sundry Search

While two leaders count the marshmallows in the last game, have oth-er leader assistants bring out two tables and set them parallel to each other on the tarp, with about four feet between the tables. Near both ends of both tables, place two aluminum pie pans. One of the pie pans should be filled with chocolate pudding, and have approximately two-dozen small chocolates submerged in it. (Try using Raisinettes or Peanut M&M's.)

Each team selects six players to participate in this game. Each of these players is given a long, plastic sundae spoon, and each team is assigned an end of a table. On the "go" signal, players have 20 sec-onds to stick the handle end of their spoons into their mouths and "search" for a chocolate candy submerged in chocolate pudding. Once found (and keeping spoon in mouth), players transfer the treat to a separate bowl. Each player gets 20 seconds to remove as many candies as possible, then a team mate takes a turn with a new spoon, until all six have participated. Award 200 chips for each transferred treasure.

Chocolate Quiz

While the MC asks more engaging questions of the audience, leaders remove the tables and props from the center, leaving the tarp in place. The following two events are great featured activities. You may opt to run either or both, depending on your group and on how much time you have. Bring out necessary props for the activity you choose to do next.

How Now Brown Cow

Get an adult volunteer from each team to come forward and sit in a chair on the tarp, facing his team. Transform these players into "cows" by having them don a brown plastic trash can liner (with head hole, of course!), a cow bell on a ribbon for around their necks, and a pair of horns (adhere a pair of horns to a headband or baseball cap.) Next to each player set two buckets – one empty one and one that contains several latex surgical gloves filled with chocolate milk and tied shut at the opening. These players will serve as "cows" and will hold the sacks of liquid while four teammates (aka, Farm Hands) "milk" the fingers! (Leaders, make sure you have several pushpins on hand for piercing the fingertips of the gloves—we do want contestants to feel success!)

   Players take turns "milking" the "Chocolate Milk" out of a latex glove into the empty bucket. Leaders should pierce the milk-gloves as the next person approaches to try his hand at milking. A cowboy hat and bandana are needed for each team to pass to the next "farm hand" as he comes forward for a turn.

Chocolate Quiz

If doing both of these activities, you will need to interject some more quiz questions for the teams while the leadership team arranges the props for this next activity.

The Great Chocolate Chip Cookie Bake-Off

One good-natured "volunteer" from each team is selected to be its "Master Chef." These players will each choose another teammate as an "apprentice." Hand each Master Chef an apron to put on and a metal or plastic mixing bowl. Announce each Master Chef in such a way that they sound highly qualified.

While one of the leadership team assistants brings out the box of cookie dough ingredients, explain, "The best way to learn the secrets of making excellent chocolate chip cookies from a Master Chef is to look over his or her shoulder."

(Assistants: Bring out stepladders, tarps, stools, box with masks, goggles, smocks, and shower caps.)

Lay out the tarp on the floor in the center of the playing area. Invite each Master Chef to don a smock, shower cap, dust mask, goggles and shower cap, then ask them to sit on a stool at the base of their team apprentice's stepladder. (Be sure to have a member of the leadership team or a trustworthy volunteer from each team alternate as ladder holders, to keep it steady throughout the activity.)

Distribute cookie ingredients to teammates who are seated in the chairs. On the "go" signal, players will take turns racing up to their team's apprentice, who will take the ingredient and drop it into the mixing bowl—which their Master Chef is holding on top of his head!

Once the ingredient has been poured into the mixing bowl, the runner may return to the team and tag off the next player, who races up with her ingredient for the cookies.

Judges should award technical merit (speed) as well as style points for this event. Make sure you thank your Master Chefs for their assistance—and give them some sort of special "thank-you" prize. (Be sure to have plenty of towels on hand for cleanup, too!)

Cool Down Events

Announce the winner for the Guess the Number of Semi-Sweets in the Jar. Also announce the team rankings, beginning with the last place team and the number of chips they earned. If possible, award a nice chocolate-y prize to the winners, and invite everyone to share some snacks—chocolate, of course!

Chocolate Quiz

Use these questions as filler between activities, especially when you need to move props in and out of the game area.

1. What town always smells like chocolate?
    A. Cocoa Beach, FL
    B. **Hershey, PA**
    C. Carmel, CA

2. White Chocolate has real chocolate in it.
    A. True
    B. **False**

3. What does "M&M" stand for?
    A. Munchy and Mouth Watering
    B. **Mars and Murrie**
    C. More and More

4. How did Hershey's Kisses get their name?
    A. Mr. Hershey's wife kissed him after she tried his tasty new candy.
    B. They were first made for Valentine's Day gifts
    C. **"Kisses" is an old name for small pieces of chocolate wrapped in foil.**

5. About how many pound of chocolate does the average person in the United States eat every year?
    A. 6
    B. **11**
    C. 18

6. Which of these things have been made out of chocolate?
    A. Jigsaw puzzles
    B. Chess set
    C. Model of a computer diskette
    D. Model of the Statue of Liberty
    E. **All of the above**

7. Would the world's largest chocolate egg have fit inside your bathroom?
    A. Sure—it was about the size of a watermelon
    B. Probably—it was about 7 feet tall.
    C. **No way—unless you have a ceiling that is 18 feet high.**

8. You would have to eat more than a dozen Hershey Chocolate Bars to get the same amount of caffeine in one cup of coffee.
   A. **True**
   B. False

9. Napoleon carried chocolate with him on his military campaigns and ate it when he needed quick energy.
   A. **True**
   B. False

10. Chocolate can cause outbreaks of acne.
    A. True
    B. **False**

11. About two ounces of milk chocolate can be poisonous to a 10-pound puppy.
    A. **True**
    B. False

12. Hershey Chocolate U.S.A. is the largest single user of almonds in the United States.
    A. **True**
    B. False

13. Hershey's main plant in Hershey, PA , uses about 1.5 million pounds of milk each day—enough to supply everyone in a city the size of Philadelphia.
    A. **True**
    B. False

14. How many Hershey's Kisses can be produced in a day?
    A. 12 million
    B. not enough
    C. **33 million**

15. In what year were Hershey's Kisses first produced?
    A. 1921
    B. **1907**
    C. 1940

16. What was the first product advertised by Hershey Foods Corporation?
    A. **Hershey's syrup**
    B. Hershey's milk chocolate bar
    C. Mr. Goodbar chocolate bar

17. About how many Hershey's Kisses are in a pound?
    A. 26
    B. 50
    C. **95**

18. About how many cows are needed to produce enough milk for one day's production at the main Hershey's plant in Hershey, PA?
    A. **50,000**
    B. 4,000
    C. 1,000

19. How many calories are in a single Hershey's Kiss?
    A. **25 calories**
    B. 50 calories
    C. 75 calories

20. How many Hershey's chocolate chips are in a pound?
    A. **About 1,000**
    B. About 500
    C. About 376

21. At what temperature does chocolate begin to melt?
    A. 65 degrees F
    B. **78 degrees F**
    C. 95 degrees F

22. How long does it take to make a Hershey's milk chocolate bar?
    A. About 17 days
    B. About 21 days
    C. **About 10 days**

23. The Mayans of Mexico used cocoa beans for currency.
    A. **True**
    B. False

24. Columbus was the first European to taste chocolate, but he was not impressed.
    A. **True**
    B. False

25. Xocoatl (pronounced chocolatl) was a cold frothy chocolate drink, mixed with honey, spices and vanilla, drunk by the Mayan Emperor Montezuma in the 16th century.
    A. **True**
    B. False

26. Mayan Emperor Montezuma drank how many goblets of chocolate drink every day?
    A. 5
    B. 25
    C. **50**

27. Before entering his harem, Mayan Emperor Montezuma would drink a golden goblet of chocolate drink then throw the goblet into a lake.
    A. **True**
    B. False

28. The Spanish Conquistador Cortes brought chocolate to Europe.
    A. **True**
    B. False

29. Cocoa comes from cacao trees.
    A. **True**
    B. False

30. Cacao trees grow how tall?
    A. 5 to 8 feet
    B. 12 to 15 feet
    C. **20 to 30 feet**

Chocolate Quiz questions have been based on the following sources:

Divone, J. (1987). *Chocolate molds: A history and encyclopedia*. Oakton, VA: Oakton Hills Publications.

Duckworth, C. (1996, February). *Ranger Rick, 30*(2), 14–15. Vienna, VA: National Wildlife Federation.

Godivia website. (n.d.). Chocolate trivia. Retrieved August 9, 2004, from http://www.godiva.com:80/resources/trivia.html

http://www.hersheys.com~hershey/fun.facts.html Retrieved January 21, 1996

http://www.hersheys.com~hershey/fun.facts2.html Retrieved January 21, 1996

Minifie, B. (1989). *Chocolate, cocoa, and confectionery: Science and technology* (3rd ed.). New York, NY: Van Nostrand Reinhold.

Morton, M. and Morton, F. (1986). *Chocolate: An illustrated history*. New York, NY: Crown Publishers.

Cupid's Quiver:
A Valentine's Day Event for
Couples

Valentine's Day is a special time for celebrating a relationship with a significant other. This program is designed to combine light-hearted, organized fun with mingling, refreshments, and dancing. Just the right mix of structure and spontaneity to please most any couple.

Atmosphere Enhancers

- Decorate the area with hearts and streamers, balloons, candles, and flowers.

- If available, borrow a fountain, some large silk or real plants, and some white, wooden lattice arches or dividers.

- Arrange six-person round tables randomly in the hall. Cover with pink, white, or red tablecloths.

- Place a centerpiece arrangement in the middle of each table. Depending on what is available to you, you may consider raffling off each of the centerpieces as a souvenir of the evening.

- Play some appropriate background music. (Anyone have a connection with a string quartet?)

Getting Ready

- Develop questionnaires to be given to couples when they register (see sample p. 79).

- Recruit a photographer.

- Print nametags for participants in advance.

- Set up sound system for background and dancing music, and for microphones for the MC and "Jay" for the Not Necessarily Newlywed Game.

- Lay out refreshments.

- Set up "paradise" photo area with palm or ficus trees and a nice background.

- Set up camera tripod and supplies for labeling the pictures.

- Write up "Who Are We?" cards for each couple on paper large enough to fold a flap over the writing. Keep pairs of cards together, so they may be given to the same couple. Ready tape or pins for adhering cards to the backs of guests. If you prefer, hole punch the cards and tie ribbon through the holes to make necklaces which can be worn on the back. This will eliminate the possibility of damaging dress and suit coat fabric.

- Develop "You Did What!?" sheets for participants. Ready pencils for each person.

- Have prize(s) ready for winner(s).

- Recruit and instruct servers, if available.

- Recruit an MC and "Jay" for the Not Necessarily Newlywed Game.

- Make banner for the game.

- Recruit someone to record answers to questions on poster-board pieces.

- Prepare at least 72 pieces of 7-inch by 11-inch posterboard. Several dark permanent markers will be needed for recording responses.

- Develop scoreboard of chalkboard or whiteboard with appropriate writing and erasing implements.

- Recruit someone to keep score and to escort contestants in and out.

- Develop list of questions to ask contestants (see samples pp. 81–84)

- Devise a means of recruiting contestants.

- Acquire a "fabulous prize" for the winning couple, and consolation prizes for the other contestant couples.

- Write a description of the "fabulous prize" and the consolation prizes for "Jay" to read.

- Set up banquet tables with pairs of chairs behind them for the contestants' "stage" area. Cover tables with tablecloths.

- Designate an auxiliary room for contestants to use as a "soundproof booth."

- Compile list of "Wonderful (Yet Inexpensive) Dates" from those shared by couples on their registration questionnaire (see sample p. 87). Have copies made for each person.

- Prepare refreshments and coffee area for guests.

Registration

- Have couples register and pay in advance. Limit the participation to those who have registered.

- Determine if couples will bring desserts/snacks to share, or if you will use ticket fees to purchase refreshments.

- When tickets are given out in advance, also give each couple a simple questionnaire (see p. 79). These should be turned in a week prior to the event.

- Prepare nametags in advance. If possible, have someone print them out on a computer or write them in calligraphy.

Group Starters

- After couples arrive, check in, and register, invite them to go into the main room. Have coffee, punch, and light finger foods for refreshments. Have candles lit and music playing when they arrive.

- Encourage couples to get their pictures taken in "paradise."

- Either use an instant developing camera and adhere labels stating the function's name and date, or get the couple's address and mail photos later, with a "thank you for attending" note.)

Mixers

You may want to select one or both of the following mixers to get Cupid's Quiver started, depending on your group and the time allowed for this portion of the event.

Who Are We?

Have couples stand together in a line. To the back of each couple, pin or tape the name of a famous couple. Write the names on pieces of paper that are folded, so one spouse may not easily observe the others' label. (Obviously, the woman should be given the woman's name; the man receives the man's name.) Examples of famous couples might be Romeo and Juliet, Lovey and Thurston Howell III, Ricky and Lucy. Participants should be instructed to give no clues as to a person's alter ego. Rather, each couple must ask yes/no questions to determine who they are. When a couple successfully discovers who they are, they may remove the labels.

You Did What?!

Based on the information couples supplied on their registration questionnaires, develop a list of wild or interesting activities couples have done. Distribute one of these sheets and a pencil to each couple. (If your group knows one another fairly well, give the couples five minutes to make their best guesses as to which other couple did each of the items listed.) Couples then mingle around, trying to determine which other couple did what. Couples may only ask, "Are you the couple that did—?" They may *not* ask couples to just tell them what they did. At the end of 10 minutes, reassemble the group, read off each activity, and have the couple who did that activity stand up and be recognized. Have couples total the number of adventures they correctly attributed to other couples, and give a small prize to the winning couple(s).

Encourage couples to follow up with others later in the evening to get more details of these interesting events. Have servers bring coffee and dessert to the tables, or allow time for couples to get refreshments.

Featured Event

The Not Necessarily Newlywed Game

This take off of the television game show is sure to be humorous and enjoyable for all! Since the object of the evening is to bring couples together and lengthen relationships, not to embarrass or humiliate them, ask questions which are innocuous and in good taste.

Depending on how well you know your group, you may want to select couples to be contestants in one of two ways. You may approach them during one of the previous mixers, or you may simply ask for a few couples to volunteer as you introduce this activity. Don't ask couples to participate too much in advance, since spontaneous and unrehearsed answers will work best for this activity.

Once you have four couples willing to participate, seat them at the "booths" you have prepared on your mock television recording set. Have the MC allow each couple to introduce themselves, tell how long they have known each other, and how they met. The MC should then explain how the game show works, and allow "Jay" to announce the fabulous prize the couples are playing for. ("Jay" should certainly embellish as much as possible, and be sure to end with the estimated retail value of the prize.) The

women are then escorted to the "soundproof" room while the men are asked questions.

The men are asked questions about their wives/significant others, or their relationship. As they respond, their answers should be written on 7-inch by 11-inch pieces of posterboard (by one of your assistants.) After all these questions are asked and answers recorded, the women are reunited with their partners. The same questions are asked of them, and their answers are compared to the responses given by the male. Points are awarded to couples for each correct answer. The men are then escorted to the "soundproof" room, and the women are asked a different set of questions. The men return, and they answer the same questions as the women were given. The final question should be a bonus question, which, if answered correctly, should be worth three times as many points as the other questions. Tally the scores, and award the grand prize. Other contestants should receive a consolation prize, and be thanked for participating.

There are several keys to success with this activity. Recruit an MC who is very humorous, spontaneous, and comfortable with this role. Select couples who you know to be of good humor as well. Prepare questions and props well in advance, to provide for a smooth presentation.

Sharing of Ideas

Explain that though not everyone had the opportunity to be contestants, they all will be receiving a consolation prize—a compilation of "Wonderful (Yet Inexpensive) Dates" provided by couples here. Encourage couples to read through (and try!) some of the ideas.

Refreshments, Mingling, Dancing

The remainder of the evening is mingling, dancing, and enjoying refreshments. Be sure to thank each couple for participating, and each assistant for helping.

Cupid's Quiver:
A Valentine's Event for Couples

We are so glad you have registered to join us! Cupid's Quiver will be a delightful evening, a combination of free-form fun and structured adult activities (no food fights or relays).

To assist us in personalizing the evening, please complete the following questionnaire, and return it by February 6.

Names: _____

Phone number or e-mail address: _____

List one or several exciting, interesting, totally bizarre, or humorous experiences you have shared as a couple.

_____

_____

_____

_____

List one or more wonderful, yet inexpensive, dates you have shared.

_____

_____

_____

_____

Thank you! We look forward to seeing you Friday, February 14, 7:00–9:30 p.m. Dress is "nice." Each couple, please bring a snack or dessert to share.

Cupid's Quiver:
A Valentine's Event for Couples

Schedule of Events

6:00	Leaders arrive, set up sound equipment, registration table, photo equipment, snack table, orient leaders to schedule/program. (Room will be decorated in the afternoon.)
7:00	Guests arrive.
7:15	Introduction to evening, welcome, distribute sheets and pencils, introduce "You Did What?!" game, introduce couples.
7:45	Reassemble, compare guesses with actual couples, prize to winning couple(s).
8:15	Not Necessarily Newlywed Game.
8:45	End of game. Award prizes, distribute "Wonderful (Yet Inexpensive) Dates" sheets, and encourage couples to share more ideas with others at their table. Play appropriate music and prompt couples to dance, mingle, enjoy more desserts.
9:30	End of Event—Cleanup.

Thank you for your help!

The Not Necessarily Newlywed Game

Questions for the Men

50 Points Each

1. Would you say your wife is more of a morning person or
    night person?

2. When you met your wife, how was she dressed?
    A. In athletic attire
    B. In casual clothes
    C. In uniform
    D. Dressed up

3. After you proposed to your wife, who was the first person she
    told?
    A. A friend
    B. Her sister/brother
    C. Her parent(s)
    D. Someone else

4. If you had to describe your wife as a car from the 1960s,
    which would she be:
    A. A tie-dyed VW microbus with peace signs painted on
        every door
    B. A 4-door Dodge Dart with a slant 6
    C. A Cadillac Coupe de Ville with landau roof and full
        Corinthian leather interior
    D. A Dodge Charger Hemi with a V8 with overhead cams and
        twice pipes

5. If you wanted to pamper
    your wife, she would most want
    you to:
    A. Bring her flowers
    B. Give her an afternoon with-
        out the kids
    C. Rub her feet
    D. Draw her a hot bath

6. If your wife couldn't go out with you on Valentine's Day, who would she most likely pick to take your place?
    A. Harrison Ford
    B. Denzel Washington
    C. Tiger Woods
    D. Billy Graham
    E. Elvis

7. If the grand prize for winning the Not Necessarily Newlywed Game were a vehicle of your wife's choosing (it's not!), which type of vehicle would your wife most likely pick:
    A. Sports car
    B. Minivan
    C. Sport utility vehicle
    D. Pick-up truck
    E. Motorcycle

8. If you had to describe your wife as a vegetable, which one would she be? (Just kidding! There's no safe answer to that one!)

9. What would your wife say is *her* favorite Winter Olympic sport?

Bonus Question (150 points)

10. If you are out at a restaurant with your wife and you ordered dessert, your wife will most likely:
    A. Order dessert also
    B. Not partake in dessert at all
    C. Not order dessert, but end up eating most of yours!

The Not Necessarily Newlywed Game

Questions for the Women

50 Points Each

1. When your husband watches television, is he more likely to:
   A. Settle on a show he wants to watch
   B. Surf the channels, regardless of what he's watching

2. If your husband were watching the Super Bowl, which would he be most interested in seeing:
   A. The game
   B. The commercials
   C. The cheerleaders

3. If your husband were to plan a week's vacation, which would he most enjoy:
   A. Going to the beach
   B. Relaxing in the mountains
   C. Vacationing at a theme park resort
   D. Staying home

4. Which will your husband say he misses most from his younger days:
   A. His physique
   B. His hair
   C. His workable joints

5. Which of your features would your husband say is your most striking:
   A. Your hair
   B. Your eyes
   C. Your smile

6. If your husband had the opportunity to change professions for one year, what profession would he most likely choose?

7. Which of the following would your husband say best describes
    your marriage relationship:
    A. Comfortable, old slippers
    B. Flashy dancing shoes
    C. Sturdy walking shoes
    D. Bare feet

8. If your husband was given $10,000 under the condition that he
    had to spend it on one of the following, which would he choose?
    A. Motorcycle
    B. State-of-the-art home entertainment system
    C. Boat
    D. Sporting equipment

Bonus Question (150 points)

9. Who kissed whom first? Did you kiss him first, or did he kiss you?

You Did What?!

Following are some exciting, interesting, humorous and/or totally bizarre experiences some of the couples here tonight have shared. Your mission as a couple is to review the stories and try to guess which couple lived through which experience. Write that couple's name on the line marked "your guess." After you have made a guess for each story, search out couples, and see if you guessed correctly. As you mingle around confirming your guesses, you may find you have made a few incorrect assumptions! You may ask a couple if two stories are theirs, then you must move on to another couple. After you have spoken to at least one other couple, you may return to one you have misjudged. The purpose of this activity is to get to know one another better, so enjoy swapping stories!

1. One of our first dates was at an amusement park at the beach. There was a ride that was essentially a "do it yourself" Ferris wheel. (Looked like a big pendulum with a counterweight.) I [*the man*] was trying VERY HARD to make the thing cycle all the way around. I discovered later that [*the woman*] was doing all that she could to keep it from cycling, because she thought we'd be hung upside-down as it flipped over. I was the sweatiest, stinkiest mess for the rest of the date. [*The woman*] of course wasn't because her efforts were more strategic than effortful.

_____   _____
Your Guess   Actual Couple

2. We went picnicking and swimming at Jordan Lake and buried our keys in the sand under our cooler so they wouldn't get stolen. Later, we gathered our things and returned to the car—only then remembering we had stashed our keys!

_____   _____
Your Guess   Actual Couple

3. One of our early dates was spent exploring a cave—then taking [*the wife*] to the emergency room for stitches!

_____   _____
Your Guess   Actual Couple

4. When we were on a cruise for our honeymoon, [*the wife*] sent her luggage to be packed away in the hold of the ship—and neglected to keep a set of clothes to put on after her shower! Fortunately, her heroic husband was able to locate their luggage and retrieve some clothes.

_____   _____
Your Guess   Actual Couple

Wonderful (Yet Inexpensive) Dates

Couples were asked to share one or more wonderful, yet inexpensive, dates they have shared together. Some could be done locally. Others may require some travel! Read the list over. Talk with your spouse about which ones you'd like to try—then set a date and plan to enjoy some special time alone together, real soon!

1. Enjoy a lobster dinner at home by candlelight.

2. Walk around the Arboretum, or a local nursery, then go for coffee and pastry.

3. Drive to a nearby historic area or quaint town for the day and enjoy the architecture, shops, and sites of historical note.

4. Spend an evening on a bookstore date.

5. Share dessert (under $5), then go to a bargain matinee.

6. Accept an invitation to someone's wedding. Enjoy the food and festivities, and reflect on how wonderful it is to be married to each other.

7. Take the kids to the YMCA, and return home for a romantic candlelight dinner.

8. Enjoy conversation at the local coffee shop.

9. Set up an impromptu picnic on the deck or back yard.

10. Take a walk in the rain and get soaking wet.

11. Four candles, one whirlpool, and two people in love.

12. Indulge at your favorite ice-cream stand.

13. Take a long "walk and talk" then order out a large soup and entree at your favorite Chinese restaurant.

14. Wander around Home Depot and pick out cabinets, carpets, whirlpools, etc.—with no intention of buying them!

15. Sit on the porch on a starry night, holding each other.

16. Curl up on the couch with a good book. Take turns reading aloud, while the other person rubs your feet.

Down on the Farm

I grew up "outside of town"—and loved it! We enjoyed fresh air, wide open spaces, and a small flock of chickens. The town has grown now, and we have moved, but I love "going back" to simpler, more rural times—even if just vicariously through a delightful program like this one. Gather up some younger kids, and let's head Down on the Farm!

Preparation

- Set up registration table with sign-in sheets and nametags. Put different animal stickers on the nametags to distinguish teams.

- Set up crafts table. Lay out white paper lunch bags, crayons, stickers, and markers. Decorate one bag so children have an example. Be sure to write the child's name on his or her bag.

- Tape eight feet of newsprint on a wall at a height the children can easily reach. Set out a bucket of crayons. Title the sheet "Down on the Farm." Add a curved line or two for rolling hills, and a barn, if you're feeling artistic. Children who arrive early add more to the scene.

- Locate several stuffed animal chickens, or something similar.

- Tennis ball or Koosh—to be used as the fox.

- Assign someone to be the Candy Meister who will distribute candy to the bags after each game.

- Purchase several large bags of small candies to put in plastic eggs and into candy bags. Purchase several large bags of "better" candy to distribute to the bags of the teams that win each relay.

- Arrange chairs in a polygon, with as many sides as you will have teams. Make sure each team has enough chairs for each member to be able to sit down.

- Fill a plastic Easter egg with a few small candies for each player, and locate a beach towel for each team.

- Each team needs a basket or sand bucket, or something similar for collecting eggs.

- Decorate the exterior of a large cardboard or plastic box with pigs. Include a stuffed animal pig in the box, if available.

- Ready 8-foot banquet tables, two teams per table.

- Each table will need a large box lid (like from a copy paper box), and two shoeboxes. Decorate the boxes if desired, so the large lids are the "gardens," and the shoeboxes are the "rabbit hutches." Set a stuffed animal rabbit next to each hutch.

- Cut 1.5-inch by 3-inch carrots out of orange paper. You will need at least six per player.

- Get drinking straws, enough for each player to have one plus a few extras.

- Place a large trashcan, with clean liner, in the center of the playing area.

- Locate a stick horse for each team, or create them by attaching construction paper or foam sheets shaped like a horse head to a broomstick or thick dowel.

- Prepare a chair for the storyteller.

- Ready a simple snack to give to the children at the end of the program.

Registration

At the registration table, have nametags for each participant, written in large block letters. Each nametag should have an animal sticker in on corner, indicating which team the child will be on.

Group Starters

Make A Basket

Each child should decorate a white lunch bag using available crayons, stickers, markers, etc. Make sure the child's name is on the bag. Have the Candy Meister mark the bags with animal stickers that match the ones on the children's nametags, and line them up somewhere out of the way, according to teams.

Farm Scene Mural

Tape a large sheet of paper to the wall, low enough so the children can reach it. Give the early arriving children crayons, and ask them to draw animals or farm scenes on the paper while they wait for the program to begin.

Mixers

Pass the Chicken

Pass a rubber (or plastic, or fabric) chicken from person to person while everyone stands in a circle in the center of the playing area. Ask each person to tell their name and a favorite farm animal. Leaders should distribute themselves among the participants in the circle to control behavior as needed.

The Fox and the Chickens

While still standing in a circle, pass toy chickens from person to person. Introduce the fox (a ball). The fox may be tossed around the circle, trying to time his arrival into someone's arms the same time a chicken gets there. If this happens, the chicken gets eaten! Play for several minutes to warm up the group to the theme and to one another.

Team Games

Each team needs an adult coach. An additional adult (the Candy Meister) needs to put candy in baskets of the winning team, and "lesser" candy in other teams' baskets. With every game, each child gets a candy prize, though they won't be given their goodie bags of candy until they are ready to walk out the door. To simplify this process, the Candy Meister could put an equal amount of small candies in each basket now, and just add the "better" candies to the winning team's baskets after each relay.

Barn Yard

Each person will have an animal sticker on her name tag. On "go" each person makes the sound of that animal, and gets together with others of her kind, forming a team. Each team is assigned one of the rows of chairs along the sides of the polygon. Have children sit in the chairs.

Wake Up! Relay

The rightmost person from each team begins. On "go" (a rooster cock-a-doodle!) the first person stands up, sits down, shakes the arm of the next person, and says "Wake up!" When the last person in line is awakened, he stands up and cock-a-doodles!

Between relay races, have the rightmost player from each team move to their team's leftmost chair, and have all the other players on the team slide one chair to the right. This will allow different children to go first each race.

Duck Waddle

Each person is given a little plastic egg to hold between his knees. On the "go" signal, each player leaves his seat waddles to the center of the square, and "lays" his egg in his team's beach towel nest, and returns to tap off the next player.

Egg Collecting Relay

Hand the rightmost player on each team a basket. Players will take turns running up to the nest to collect one egg. While the first child is running up to the nest, the rest of the team shifts one seat to the right, leaving an empty seat at the left end of the row. Once the first player has an egg in the basket, she returns to the end of her line, takes out the egg, and passes the empty basket up to the new first person in line. After all teams have finished, everyone may open her egg, and eat the candy, but have the children hold onto those eggshells for the next event.

Pig Slop Relay

Each player now gets a chance to run her egg-shells up to the pigpen. (Place a box in the center of the square. Line the box with one or more of the beach towel "nests" to minimize egg breakage.) Have players "feed" their eggshells to the (stuffed animal) pig, then race back to their places in line to tap off the next pig sloppers.

Feed the Bunnies

Set long tables in the middle of the square. Two teams will use the same table. Place a large box lid (the garden) at one end, and two shoeboxes with bunnies at the other end of each table. Each player is given a clean straw. When it is her turn, she comes to the center, in-hales deeply, sucking up a paper carrot from the "garden" and walks it down to the "bunny hutch," exhaling to let the carrot fall into the shoebox. Each team's competitors get 30 seconds to feed as many car-rots as they can to their "bunny" before returning to the end of their team's line. Continue until each player has taken a turn feeding the bunny. Count the number of carrots each team feeds their bunny / shoebox. The champion team is the one with the best fed rabbit!

Horse Feed

Most horses eat hay, but ours like "straws." (Get it!?) In turn, farmers race up to the center of the corral, and contribute their straws [from the last game] to the feed trough (large trash can), then return to the line and tap off the next farmer, until all have fed their straws.

Barrel Racing Relay

The first person in each line is given a "horse" (a construction-paper-headed broom or dowel). She straddles the horse, rides it to the center of the playing area, circles halfway around the barrel, keeping her left shoulder near the barrel, and returns to the end of her team's line. The horse gets carefully passed person to person to the next ready rider. Other team members should shift right into the empty chair while the "rider" is out racing. Racing continues until the first person is back in her original seat.

Cool Down

Animal Story

Have children sit with their teams on the floor, in front of the storyteller. When the name of each animal is mentioned in the story, instruct that team to make its noise. Have the storyteller relate a story about how all the animals thought they were the best kind of animal. The animals all boast, "You're not cool unless you're MY kind of an animal." Conclude with the Wise Farmer assuring each type of animal that they are special and valuable for who they are.

Snack

While everyone is still sitting in their teams, adults serve snacks to the children. Children should stay settled until their parents/guardians come for them.

Thank You

Thank each child for participating, and each parent for allowing her child to attend. Remember to give out the bags of candy, and to thank your staff for their role in facilitating the fun!

Game Show Gala

Television game shows look so easy, seemingly anyone could win. They also look like a lot of fun. The games in this Game Show Gala are designed to be both fun and easy to win, because it is so much fun to win! Ask participants to dress in flamboyant clothes (à la TV game show *Let's Make a Deal*), assuring the evening's excitement will begin right away.

This is a relatively complex program, which requires a lot of props, preparations, and volunteer assistance. But, it is well worth the effort! Read through the chapter to get a good understanding of what is involved. Modify the games and prizes to suit your group, but by all means, give this one a try (it may just become an annual event for your group).

Set Up

Arrange chairs in slanted "U" formation, with the stage in the center top. Allow for 15–20 feet of additional stage area before placing the row of curtains. Have game props and prizes labeled and ready backstage, with several people serving as stage crew.

A sound system is critical to the success of this program, as is the selection of an appropriate someone to be "The Voice" of the announcer. To best prepare the announcer, have him watch several episodes of game shows on TV, making notes of key phrases and vocal inflections.

Staff/Roles

Blob Blarker   host of The Price is Right

Jay   the Announcer, with a dramatic, exaggerated voice

Laura   the Lovely Assistant, who marks down contestants' bids, brings out props, and shows off prizes

Other Lovely Assistants	also bring out props and show off prizes
Warm-Up Person	gets the crowd worked up and ready to begin the game shows; provides filler between shows
Prompter	explains to the audience the "proper" way to cheer and applaud, "helps" contestants by giving them "advice" (posters with prompting messages are helpful)
Honty Mall	host of Let's Make a Deal.
Back Stage Director and Assistants	make sure all game props and prizes are ready and in the proper place for use during the game
Greeters	several people who sign people in, and write up and hand out nametags.
Store Proprietors	in charge of exchanging the play money given out for "valuable prizes."

Store

Throughout the evening, play money will be given out. Participants may want to keep some as souvenirs. More likely, though, they will want to spend it at your "store."

Have an area set up ahead of time to be your store. On the wall behind the store, display a sample of what can be purchased, according to price. This will allow those waiting in line to decide what they want before they get to the front of the line.

Items need not be elaborate or expensive. For example, $100 play money would buy you a Reese's Peanut Butter Cup, or a pack of gum. $300 might get you a fancy pencil or a Fruit Roll-Up. For $500, you could purchase a King Size Kit Kat bar or a highlighter. A box of microwave popcorn, a two-liter bottle of soda, or a flashlight with batteries could be sold for $1000 play money. In general, though, the fewer the choices they have at each price category, the more quickly they will be able to decide what to purchase. Make sure you have plenty of items on hand, especially in the lower price range.

The quantity, quality, and type of prizes will depend on what is appropriate for the audience, and on how much money you intend to give out during the evening, especially at the end of Let's Make a Deal. Also, consider the amount of money you are charging for the program. The more you charge, the nicer the prizes should be. Check with local merchants for donations or discounts.

Games

The games listed here are a representative sampling of the types of games
played on these shows. Do not feel
limited to use these exclusively. Make
up your own, or watch the shows
for more ideas. The prizes given out
are also samples. Use what is readily
available to you, especially if prizes
can be donated by individuals or
merchants. Select prizes appropriate
to your audience, considering their
age and interests.

Arrival Activities

As participants arrive, they are welcomed by Greeters with clipboards in hand. On numbered paper, Greeters take down the people's names and note any interesting things about them, such as costumes, props, or flamboyancy. Participants are given large, price tag-like nametags, and invited to move into the stage area.

Preshow Warm Ups

Select a vivacious person (to warm up the crowd) whose responsibilities include the following:

- Explaining the evening's activities, suggesting strategies to being selected to participate, and how to use the "money" they win.

- Instructing the audience on how to respond to given visual and oral commands (e.g., applause, cheer, oooh, ahhh, offering advice to contestants). You may want a designated Prompter to do this now, and also do the actual prompting during the show.

- Further engaging the crowd by telling jokes, leading crazy audience participation songs/chants, doing some warm-up games with the group.

- Giving out some prizes, thus building the "need to win a prize" frenzy.

- Building up excitement for the first game show, so the host is welcomed with frantic applause.

The Price Is Right

After due fanfare, the Announcer introduces "The host of our show, Blob Blarker!" (Especially good if you have a large host!) Blob welcomes everyone, then asks "Jay" (the Announcer) who the first contestants will be.

"Cindy Pletcher, come on down! You're the first contestant on The Price is Right!" Jay continues calling people down one at a time, until there are four contestants standing at podium at the front of the stage.

Have a markerboard on an easel beside the contestants, with a Lovely Assistant ready to take down the contestant's guess next to their name. Of course, if you happen to have the electronic equipment and know-how to duplicate the podiums they use on TV, great! Otherwise, use the inexpensive alternative described here.

Blob then asks, "Jay, what is the first item up for bid?"

Jay then describes the item about which contestants will try to guess the actual retail price (without going over). After reiteration of the rules for guessing (actual retail price without going over), Blob invites the first contestant to make a guess. The lovely assistant, Laura, writes the amount next to the person's name on the markerboard. (When contestants are being called down, Laura should write their first names on the left side of the markerboard.) This continues until all four contestants have given a different guess. (No two people may give the same guess.)

On a slip of paper, both Blob and Jay will have the name of the item and its actual retail price. If all contestants have guessed over the actual retail price, Jay will sound a buzzer from the sound table. If the buzzer is not sounded, Blob will announce, "The actual retail price is ___. The closest bid is from Cindy. Come on up and play our first game."

Game One: Proper Order

Blob   Jay, tell Cindy what she is playing for.

Jay   Blob, it's a NEW CAR!

Open Curtain #1 to reveal a car poster, a toy car, or a real car, if you can get it in the building! In the case of the real car, be sure to have a sign sitting in front of it which says, "Management reserves the right to substitute prizes!" And have a Matchbox car ready for them. Jay then proceeds to describe the car. While everyone is "ooohing and ah-hhing" (as prompted), Laura brings out the props for the game.

Blob   On the board are five digits, which are all in the correct price of the car. Your job, Cindy, is to place the numbers in the proper order to give us the actual retail price of the car. As long as you have at least one digit in the proper place, you can continue playing the game.

Cindy manipulates the numbers until she thinks the price is right. Warm-up person and others encourage audience participation in providing advice to the contestant. When Cindy has completed making her first guess, Blob instructs her to ask the judges, "Judges, do I have at least one number correct?" If the answer is yes, the judges (Jay or others) ring a bell. Cindy continues to ask, "Judges, do I have two (three, four...) numbers correct?" until the judges buzz her with a buzzer. Once Cindy knows how many numbers she has incorrect, she may switch that many digits, and ask the judges again how she is doing. Hopefully, the contestant will eventually place the numbers in the correct order, allowing her to win the car (or a substitute prize) and some "cash" for gasoline money. If Cindy is unsuccessful in having even one digit correct, Blob gives her a $100 consolation prize, and she sits down.

To maximize involvement of participants, have contestants sit back down if they did not win the bid. Or, to make it more like the real show, have them stay up, and just get one replacement contestant. Laura wipes the markerboard clean between rounds.

Blob Jay, get us another contestant (or group of contestants). (Jay invites another one (four) contestant(s) to "come on down!") Let's see what the next item up for bid is.

Laura opens the curtain or wheels out the next item up for bid. Note: These items are not given away, so you could use most anything readily available. Just write up a description of it for Jay, and come up with a purchase price for it. Jay describes the item.

Beginning with the newcomer, Blob asks contestants to give their bid on the actual retail price of the item, without going over it. Again, Laura writes the bids down on the marker board next to the contestant's name. Once a contestant has been selected, he bounds up to Blob, amid the cheers and applause of the audience, to play the next game.

Game Two: Shopping Spree

Laura opens Curtain #2 to reveal a table set with items.

Blob Before you are 10 items typically found in a grocery store. What you need to do is select 5 of these items, so they total up to $15. You don't want to spend more than $15 on these items. But if you can select 5 items without going over $15, you will win $1,000. Jay, tell us about the items Joe has to choose from.

Jay then proceeds to describe each of the items (humorously). (Items could include: box of cereal, bottle/box of laundry detergent, household cleanser, TV dinner, bag of chips, half gallon of milk, multi-pack of toilet paper. Most items should be worth about $2 to $3 each. A few should be in the $3 to $5 range.)

Set Up

Arrange items on the table with plenty of room between them. In front of each item, place a placard with the actual price on it, face down. Once Jay has described the items, Blob invites the contestant to select the first item. Blob then turns over the placard, revealing the item's price. Be sure the Prompter encourages the audience to "help" Joe, by screaming out items he should select. This continues, with Blob keeping a running tally of how much money the contestant has "spent." As long as Joe is within the $15 limit, each time the placard is flipped over, the Judge should ring the bell. If an item pushes Joe over the $15 mark, the Judge sounds an ominous buzzer. (Fog horn would be great, if available.) If Joe is successful in his challenge, he wins $1,000 play money, or a "valuable" prize. If he is unsuccessful, he receives a $100 consolation prize.

Game Three: The Range Game

As before, select contestants, and have them bid on the next item to see which one gets to play the next game. If desired, you may have all four come up and play.

Blob   Jay, let's hear what this contestant could win, if the Price is Right!

Laura opens the curtain, revealing the prize for this game, while Jay explains it. He does NOT tell it's actual retail price. The Range Instrument is also wheeled out to the middle of the stage.

Blob hands the contestant(s) a 5-inch by 8-inch card with his or her name on it. The contestant places it on the Range Instrument, covering a $1 range (or more, depending on the prize), in which he or she believes the item's price falls. If one contestant is playing, the range should be wider than if four play, to give the single contestant a better chance of winning. (if all four contestants are playing, allow them to place their card on the Range Instrument one at a time. Cards may touch each other, but they may not overlap.) If playing with four contestants, the Judge sounds a buzzer if none of the cards is covering the price. One at a time, they may move their card.

Once the guesses are set, the sliding arrow on the Range Instrument is moved to the item's actual retail price. (Play some suspenseful music (like the theme from *Jaws*) while the arrow is being moved.)

When the arrow stops, the Judge rings the bell, and Blob gives the actual retail price, and declares a winner. In the case of a single contestant who does not win, Blob offers his condolences and $100 to the contestant.

The Mega Showcase

Two contestants are needed for this event. Select two previous big winners (or losers), or call in two brand new contestants. The two contestants stand behind podiums, as the earlier contestants did. The first curtain is drawn back, revealing the first showcase.

Amid the "oooh's and ahhh's" Jay describes the package. The first contestant has the option to bid on that showcase, or pass it to the other contestant. One gives what they believe is the value of that showcase.

The second showcase is then unveiled and described. Whichever contestant did not bid on the first one bids on this showcase.

Once both bids have been recorded by Laura on the marker board, Blob quickly calculates the difference between guessed prices and actual retail prices. (Or have someone backstage use a calculator to figure this out, and just hand Blob a note with the price differences, with the closer one circled.) Blob gives the actual retail price of the first showcase, reiterates the contestant's bid on it, and announces the difference. He does this with the second showcase, then declares the one whose bid was the closest as the winner.

Everyone cheers, and Jay runs through the end-of-show credits: Travel arrangements have been made by _____ ...a promotional fee has been paid by _____ ...a proud sponsor of _____.

Sample Showcases

Note: Items with (*) are what the winner actually gets to take home.

Entertainment Center

- Inexpensive personal CD player (with batteries)*
- Videocassette tape or DVD*
- TV/VCR/DVD player from center/someone's house
- Boom box (borrowed)

- Comfortable chair/recliner/couch
- Box of microwave popcorn (plus extra bag, popped, for model to munch on!)*
- Microwave oven (from staff lounge)

Beach Vacation

- Patio/beach chairs
- Beach umbrella
- Cooler*
- Six-pack of soda*
- Bag of chips*
- Beach bucket, shovel, beach ball*
- Inner tube/float*
- Travel poster(s) of Hawaii (which Jay can emphasize in such a way as to make casual listener think the winner may actually get a *trip* there!)*

Break

During the break, the stage crew changes game show sign or banner, and moves the next game's props and prizes into position.

Keeping in line with the television counterparts, plug in a commercial or two that some volunteers have worked up. Remind the group where the rest rooms and concession stand are located. Warm-up person returns to give any special instructions for the second game show, and generally fires the group up for making some deals!

The Price Is Right: Backstage Info

Game One: First Item Up For Bid, Casio Keyboard

Have Model take it out from very end of curtain, behind palm tree. Model should play demo music. Once contestants begin bidding, Model takes keyboard back. She should stand on the side of the stage until it is time to pull back Curtain #1.

Game One: Proper Order

Once a contestant has been selected, Blob will say, "Jay, what is our contestant playing for?" As soon as Jay begins speaking, two models should pull back (and hold open) Curtain #1.

Prior to the event, write or type each of the five digits of the price of the car on an 8x10 sheet of paper (one digit per sheet) and slip them into acrylic 8x10 frames. Set the frames on a table, which the props crew will bring out through Curtain #2.

After the contestant finishes playing the game (and presumably wins!), the table with the props needs to be moved backstage, out of the way. The prop should be removed from the table, so Range Finder (for Game #3) can be placed on it. The table with props for Game #2 needs to be moved into ready position behind Curtain #2.

Game Two: Item up for Bid, Hoover Convertible Vacuum

Have Model wheel it out from edge of curtain near the Palm Tree. Model should remain out front demonstrating it until the bidding starts, then return it to edge of curtain. Model should return backstage and move to Curtain #3, ready to bring out prize.

Game Two: Shopping Spree

As soon as Blob has a contestant selected, two people need to carry out the table with the props from Curtain #2.

Two Models should be ready behind Curtain #3 to carry out table, and display items as suggested on p. 102. Face down in front of each item should be its retail price marked on 4x6 index cards and placed in 4x6 acrylic frames.

Once the game is over, the table should be removed from stage, and stashed in back. Tall cart with Game #3 props/prizes should be wheeled into ready position behind Curtain #2. Range finder should also be moved onto table behind Curtain #2. (Marker and name sheets, too.)

Game Three: The Range Game

As Jay begins calling Kids' names to "come on down," someone should write each child's name in large letters on a neon orange card.

When Blob calls for it, Model should roll the tall cart with prizes on it out through Curtain #2 for Rob to describe. Once described, cart should be left on stage, and table with Range Finder should be brought out next to it, through Curtain #2. Meanwhile, backstage, showcase items should be assembled behind Curtain #2 (the Beach Vacation) and Curtain #3 (the Entertainment Center). At Blob's prompting, Model will be needed to *slowly* move Range Finder to proper price, as indicated by the dinging bell. After Winner is declared, all props should be removed from stage.

The Showcases

First Showcase: Curtain #3 Entertainment Center

Two contestants will be called up. Curtain #3 should be the First Showcase up for bid. (the Entertainment Center). Arrange so couch, TV/VCR are visible, Walkman and tape on couch for model to hold up and pretend to use. Second model comes in with bag of popped popcorn, and microwave oven needs to be wheeled in also.

Second Showcase: Curtain #2 Beach Vacation

Model sits on beach chair, under umbrella, with beach "toys" around, pulls out picnic basket to show items in it. On cue from Jay, other Model brings out posters, AAA tour book of Hawaii. Once contestants have both bid, curtains are closed. When a winner of one of the showcases has be determined, that showcase's "keeper" items can be boxed up for them. The other showcase needs to remain "intact" for final event of Let's Make a Deal.

Let's Make a Deal

Jay   These contestants came from all over the world to America's marketplace: Let's Make a Deal! And here is our host: Honty Mall! (Wild cheering from audience!)

Honty walks through the audience, but stays with them to select players for the games.

Game One: What's in the Envelope?

Honty hands a sealed envelope to each of three people, who stand. Honty instructs them not to open the envelope. (Envelopes should be discretely marked so Honty knows how much is in each envelope when he hands them out.)

Honty Each of these envelopes contains at least $100 in play money. (To first contestant:) Would you like what is in the envelope, or what is behind Curtain #1 ?

   While the contestant is deliberating, the audience should be prompted to give "advice." Once the contestant has made up her mind, Honty says, "Let's see what is behind Curtain #1." (it is revealed, and Jay describes it, including its actual retail price.) Honty then instructs the contestant to open her envelope to see what she traded away for cash, or for what she passed up behind the curtain. The audience applauds while she sits back down. Honty proceeds in a like manner with the second contestant and Curtain #2.
   The first two contestants had either $100 or $500 in their envelopes. One of the prizes should be "good" and the other a "dud."

When Honty begins to deal with the third contestant, he tells her that her envelope contains twice as much money as one of the other two envelopes (either $200 or $1,000). He then gives her the option of choosing the envelope or Curtain #3. After the contestant decides, Honty has the prize behind the curtain displayed, then the envelope (which has $1,000 in it).

Game Two: This or That

Honty approaches another three members of the audience, who stand. To the first contestant, Honty hands a $500 bill.

Honty How would you like this $500? Would you like it better than what is behind is behind Curtain #1?

While contestant decides which option she prefers, the audience should shout out their opinion of the better option. If the contestant selects the money, Curtain #1 should remain closed. If she selects Curtain #1, Jay should describe what is behind the curtain, including its actual retail price.

If the first contestant selects Curtain #1, Honty hands the $500 bill to the second contestant, and makes the offer to exchange that "money" for what is behind Curtain #2. As with the previous player, either one may be selected, but Curtain #2's contents are not revealed until the third contestant has the opportunity to choose either the money or what is behind Curtain #3 (if contestant has opted for contents of Curtain #2) or Curtain #2 (if the second contestant opted for the money). (Curtain # 3 should conceal a decent prize, while Curtain #2 contains a dud prize.) Honty should reveal the prize behind the "good" curtain first, then the dud. If one of the contestants selected the curtain with the dud prize, Honty should give him a $100 consolation prize.

Game Three: The Big Deal!

Two contestants are chosen to play this game. Three curtains conceal three prizes, "totalling over $ ____ in prizes." In turn, contestants choose one of the curtains. The "best" prize is not revealed until the end. If it was not chosen, Jay describes the other two prizes for their winners, then what neither of them selected. If the "best" prize was selected, the prize package behind the curtain not selected by either contestant is first revealed and described. Next, the lesser prize package that was chosen is unveiled and described. The best prize is revealed last.

Honty summarizes who won what in the Big Deal, and invites everyone back to the next show of "Let's Make a Deal." With a pocket full of $100 play money bills, Honty moves through the audience, offering "$100 to the first person in this row who can show me a hard boiled egg" or a photo of their spouse, a plastic toy, a crossword puzzle. Honty continues making deals until time or money runs out. Jay should thank the audience for attending; and should direct them to the "store" or refreshment area.

Thank you! Good night!

Let's Make a Deal: Backstage Info

Create large circles out of fabric or posterboard with numbers 1, 2, and 3. Attach them to their respective curtains. Each of the three games require prizes be behind each of the three curtains. For each of the games, one of the curtains should conceal a "dud" or less valuable prize. The prize selections should be appropriate for your group and for your budget.

Game One: What's in the Envelope?

Prepare three envelops, one containing $100, one with $500, and one with $1000 of play money. Discreetly label each of the envelopes with a sticker or symbol. Give Honty a 3x5 card which contains the key to which envelope holds which amount of money, so he can be sure to hand the third contestant the envelope with the $1000. The "dud" prize should be behind Curtain #3.

Game Two: This or That?

In an envelope marked "Game Two: This or That?" place $500. Prepare prizes to be placed behind each of the three curtains. The "dud" prize should be behind Curtain #2.

Game Three: The Big Deal

Again, prizes are needed behind each of the curtains. One of the prizes should be the leftover showcase from The Price is Right, one a "dud" and one an "average" prize. Give Honty a 3x5 card indicating which prize is behind which curtain. Place a dozen or more $100 bills in an envelope for Honty to distribute after the "show" has ended.

Setting up the Store

Toward the back of your audience area, set out tables to make an L-shaped store counter. Behind this, set an additional table (against the wall) to serve as your back stock area. On the wall above this, place large sheets of posterboard with the items you have available and what the "price" is for each. (See note at beginning of chapter regarding types of items you may want to have for sale.) Be sure to recruit a number of volunteers to assist with sales, keeping in mind that families with young children may want to move quickly through the purchasing process, to get the children home to bed.

The Great Mall Scavenger Hunt

Experiencing the rainiest summer on record? Is your group getting tired of seeing the same four walls of your meeting place? Here's a great event you can conduct, even if you don't have your own facility: a shopping mall scavenger hunt.

Preparations

Be sure to check with mall management and get their permission to conduct this program before you start advertising this event. Most management firms are happy for you to promote their mall in this way—especially if you assure them up front that participants will be instructed to be courteous mall users.

Formulating the preliminary scavenger hunt list may be as much fun for you as the event itself! Grab a coworker or friend and head down to the designated mall during an off-peak time, such as when the stores open on a weekday. Systematically walk through the mall, jotting down possible items on a tablet of paper. Number the items as you go. If you can get a directory and map of the mall, mark these item numbers on the map for later reference. (When you finalize your list, you will probably want to have your contestants use as much of the mall as possible.) You'll probably feel like some kind of spy or undercover agent as you roam about in search of the quintessential scavenger hunt queries and quests. Have a blast!

Target the actual search portion of the event to last 45–60 minutes. The sample given was used with mixed aged teams of five to seven members, in a mall of over a million square feet. Teams took approximately 60 minutes to complete the list. Adjust your list to match your group, the size of the mall you will be using, and the intricacy of the items on the list.

Materials Needed

- Permission slips, especially if the event will involve children. Participant signatures indicate they understand and agree to abide by the conduct guidelines you describe.

- Clipboard, pen or pencil, and item list (one per team).

- List of team members (to be kept at headquarters), along with the permission slips.

- Someone on each team should have a watch, synchronized with one at headquarters.

- Team identification material: Lengths of different colors of surveyor's tape, nametags with team identification mark, visors, whatever might be appropriate for your group, if desired.

If you elect to have some items require a purchase of merchandise, participants need to be informed to bring money. (You may opt to arrange to purchase gift certificates from store managers for the specific amount of money needed at particular stores. Each team can be issued these store-specific gift certificates along with their item list. This way no one individual assumes—or gets stuck with—financial responsibility for the whole team.)

Planning Particulars

When your group arrives at the designated starting area, have them organize themselves into teams of 5 to 10 players. Teams should have approximately the same number of members on each. If your group is of mixed ages or abilities, require diversity within each team. It's no fair pitting a savvy group of agile, mall going "professionals" against a group consisting of preschoolers and mall-phobics. Besides, competition is often more fun when the teams are evenly matched.

An obvious safety point: Every team which has children on it should also have at least one responsible adult member. A 1:1 or 1:2 or 1:3 ratio is ideal, depending on the ages and manageability of the children.

Once teams have been assigned and assembled, hand out the sheet of rules and review them (see "Guidelines for Fun and Safety"). Stress the importance of group safety and courtesy toward merchants and toward other mall users.

Once all comments are given, and all questions addressed, it is time to issue the scavenger hunt list to each of the teams (see sample lists, pp. 116–118).

Bring along a camera to take candids of the group as they venture around the mall. Be sure to leave a couple of people at headquarters in case groups return early with questions, problems, or a completed scavenger hunt sheet. When teams reassemble, have a team of judges review each of their sheets and items to determine a winning team. Have an appropriate prize to award members of the winning scavenger hunt team (e.g., mall gift certificate).

Guidelines for Fun and Safety

We're glad you joined us this evening!
On with the rules for the feature event...

1. Teams will consist of five to seven players, with at least one child (if children are included) per team.

2. If your team chooses, you may split into two search parties for part of the adventure, but no one may work alone.

3. Children must have a responsible adult team member with them at all times.

4. Not everyone considers the mall a play area—some people actually *work* here. Be courteous to employees and respectful of their stores.

5. Running is not permitted while at the mall.

6. Watch out for mall shoppers—some people take their outings to the mall quite seriously (unlike us!).

7. No one may leave the mall without checking in at headquarters.

8. Meet back at headquarters at 8:30 p.m. whether you have completed the list or not.

Sample Mall Scavenger Hunt "Find" List

- What six different vegetable soaps can you get at Bath and Body Works?

- How much does a pound of red licorice cost at Gypsy's Candyland?

- What symbol is between "Team" and "Spirit"?

- What is item "D" on page 957 of the 2004 Annual Sears Catalog?

- In Suncoast Motion Picture Company, whose picture is on the far left of the "Comedy" wall?

- What do you have to do to rent a stroller at the Mall?

- Are small Beanie Babies cheaper at Fluff 'N Stuff, or at the Beanie Babies kiosk? How much cheaper?

- If you stand at the Klutz display in the Great Outdoor Provision Company, what poster is on the wall at Magnetic North?

- How much does a stuffed whole pizza from Sbarro cost?

- Which place can make you a special order, heart-shaped cookie faster, The Great American Cookie Company, or The Original Cookie?

- What denomination(s) of paper money does the Cyber Station token machine take, and how many tokens can you get for each?

- How much is a beard trim at Mitchell's?

- What kind of cash register computers do they use at Radio Shack?

- What is item "C" on page 758 of the 2004 J. C. Penney Spring/Summer Catalog?

- What stickers are on the window of store #1 ?

- The Durham Bulls'opening game is on (date) against what team?

- What is the name of the restaurant in Hudson Belk?

- What is located on the top shelf of the rightmost GNC refrigerator?

- What is at 150 degrees W Latitude, and 60 degrees N Longitude?

- When did Charles Babbage live?

- What is the phone number for the U.S. Army Recruiting Station?

- What is between Daughtry Jewelry and Allen Montague Collectors Gallery?

- How late could one stay at Spinnaker's lounge on a Sunday evening?

- What kind of cash machine is in the Food Court?

- What is the phone number of one of the pay phones outside of Thom McAn Shoes?

Sample Mall Scavenger Hunt "Do" List

- Buy a pack of gum or a small candy item. Have the cashier initial the back of your receipt.

- Buy a sheet of tissue paper from the Hallmark Store. (Choose a "good" color!)

- On the back of an "I Can't Believe It's Yogurt" napkin, write the flavors of the day from the far right machine.

- Get a straw from Chick-Fil-A.

- Buy a fortune cookie.

- Get the shoe size of everyone in your group at a shoe store using their foot measurer. Write the names and sizes on a bag, receipt, business card or anything else identifying the store. (Remember to be polite and discrete!)

- Put someone on the mailing list at the Family Bookstore.

- Buy $2 worth of your group's favorite candy from a corner candy store. (Save the receipt in case the candy gets eaten!)

- Have the smallest person in your group sit next to "Ronald McDonald" at the food court. Ask someone who is not in your group to initial to verify.

- Buy something "special" from the Dollar Store.

Mall Mania: The Fun Continues

Try this: a scavenger hunt in reverse. Instead of collecting things, you give them away!

A local grocery store chain sells carnations for 25 cents a stem, twice a year. When they do, we buy up an armful, and head to the mall. If your local market doesn't do this, contact a flower distributor for bulk prices. (You'll get better prices if you avoid major flower buying holidays, such as Mother's Day and Valentine's Day.)

Divide your group up into teams of four to six players, give them a copy of the Flower Power sheet, a pencil, and at least 24 flowers. (Groups of youths should also have at least one adult team member.) Have them give a flower to someone who fits the "description" listed, and ask the person to initial on the corresponding line. The last two "descriptions" your team may make up. Groups should be required to stay together for this event.

To "legitimize" your flower peddling, you may want to print slips of paper to distribute with your flowers, explaining who your group is, and why you are handing out free flowers to people at the mall. Include your agency name and phone number. Instruct the group *not* to take money for the flowers!

Do tell the group when and where to meet back up once teams have distributed their flowers. (Be sure to print this information on the bottom of the sheet, so they don't forget!)

Flower Power: A Reverse Scavenger Hunt!

Give a flower to: _____.
Recipient initials next to item.

1. The mother of a newborn.

2. A kiosk worker who has no customers.

3. A mall store worker.

4. A child who is 3 or 4 years old.

5. An older man or woman.

6. Someone who looks like they could use a flower.

7. A redhead.

8. A couple.

9. A teenager.

10. A person from another culture or country.

11. Someone who works in the Food Court.

12. Someone who is eating alone.

13. A man with a beard or moustache.

14. A lady with a fancy dress.

15. Someone wearing lots of earrings.

16. Someone who is reading alone.

17. An employee working frantically.

18. A mother with 3 boys.

19. (You choose)

20. (You choose)

Remember: Meet at the fountain outside Hudson Belk at 8:30 p.m.

Pumpkin Party

There's so much more to do with pumpkins than just carve them or turn them into pie. As fall approaches and pumpkins begin piling up at your local farmer's market, plan this event for the kids and young families you know. It's sure to change the way you look at pumpkins.

Getting Ready

- Decorate your area with bales of straw, pumpkins, corn, colorful fall leaves, and other autumn decorations.

- Set up a registration table with sign-in sheets and pumpkin-shaped nametags. Set out pens and permanent markers.

- Set out a jar with candy in it, with paper and pen for guesses. (Be sure to count the number of candies in the jar first!)

- Ready "goodie bag" decorating table with paper lunch bags, markers, crayons, and stickers.

- Locate a small plastic or real pumpkin (with stem removed) for passing.

- Inflate large (12-inch) orange balloons for relays. With a permanent marker, draw "happy" jack-o'-lantern faces on each. Place balloons in trash can liner. Inflate a few more than the number of teams you have, just in case.

- Ready oranges, one per team, plus one or two extras.

- Assemble chairs in a square so each team has enough for each team member per side. (Your square may actually be a pentagon if you have five teams.)

- Ready marshmallows for tossing. Locate as many small trash cans as you have teams.

- Prepare a paper or plastic bowl with pumpkin shaped candy for each team. Cover and set aside.

- Ahead of time, cut large pumpkin shapes out of orange construction paper. Have enough for one half to three quarters of your participants. Adhere them to a nonpainted or papered wall, window, or table. Set out washable markers, and invite participants to decorate them as jack-o'-lanterns after they have decorated their goodie bags, time permitting.

- Select lively music for the Musical Pumpkins game and test the sound system. Try to locate "Turkey in the Straw" or some other lively song for the last activity.

- Each team will need a metal iced tea spoon (long handle with small "scoop") and two cereal bowls. One bowl should be empty, the other bowl should be filled with pumpkin seeds.

- Locate one or two 6-foot or 8-foot banquet tables for use in Pumpkin Seed Transport Challenge and for Pumpkin Pie Feed.

- Cut pumpkin pie into slices, so each team has a slice. If your participants are small, you may need to cut smaller pieces. Place each piece on a plate, cover and set aside. Ready plastic spoons and plenty of napkins.

- Locate or make two blindfolds per team for Pumpkin Pie Feed.

- Refrigerate aerosol cans of whipped topping until needed.

- Have one or more bales of straw ready for scattering into a pile for Pumpkin in the Straw.

- Ready individually wrapped candy, gum and small prizes for scattering in the straw shortly before the game. Plan for approximately 10–12 treats per child.

- Have little pumpkin related prizes for the winning team, like pumpkin shaped peanut butter cup candies or a small pumpkin to take home and decorate.

Registration and Nametags

As your young guests arrive, have parents sign them in at the registration table and pick up a nametag for each child. Make sure first names are written in large, easy to read block letters. Have a member of your leadership team escort them to the Group Starters area and get them involved in these activities.

Group Starters

Guess the Number of Pumpkin-Shaped Candies

Assist the children as they try to guess the correct number of candies in the jar. Write their names and guesses on the sheet of paper supplied.

Decorate Paper Bags

After the children guess the number of candies, direct them to the crafts table. Give each child a white paper lunch bag, and have him decorate it with the stickers, markers, and crayons provided. Make sure each child has his name on the bag, so it can be returned to him at the end of the event—with candy in it!

Jack-o'-Lantern Coloring

If children finish decorating their bags and still have time before the mixers begin, invite children to decorate "blank" jack-o'-lantern cutouts and display.

Mixers

Welcome! Once the participants have arrived, gather the group into a large circle and welcome them to Pumpkin Party! Introduce yourself and the leadership team.

Pumpkin Name Pass

Pass a small pumpkin from person to person, having each participant loudly say his or her name.

Line-Up

With assistance of the leadership team, have the children line up smallest to tallest. If your group is rather large, you may need to swing the line around to form a circle.

Pumpkin Pass Challenge

Challenge the group to pass the small pumpkin down the line and back as quickly as possible. If your watch has a second hand, time the group's effort. Run one or two more trials to set a group record.

Team Dividing

Separate into teams by counting off by the number of teams you want. Allow for 8–12 players per team.

Team Games

While teams are doing the relay races, have a member of the leadership team line the decorated bags up alphabetically, and fill each with candy. These will be handed back to the children when they leave the event.

Pumpkin Relay

With teams lined up relay style, hand each team an orange balloon, on which you have drawn a happy jack-o'-lantern face. Have teams race by passing the balloon down the line and back. After each race, have the first person in each line move to the back of their lines.

Pass the Pumpkins Relay

Continue with more pumpkin passing variations: between legs, overhead, over, under.

> **Leaders:** Keep the focus of these races on going fast, getting faster as a team, encouraging one another, and having fun! Team prizes will not be given out at the end. Everyone will receive a goodie bag of treats for participating, so keep the enthusiasm and affirmations running high.

Pass the Pumpkin

Participants pass a "pumpkin" (orange) under the chin down the line.

Popping Pumpkins

Pumpkin shaped candy in bowls are passed down the line. The last person takes the bowl, runs to other end, eats a candy, and sends the bowl back down the line.

Musical Pumpkins

When music stops, children must run and stand on pumpkin shape which has been cut out of construction paper and taped to the floor. Keep rounds short, so the game moves quickly for those who have been eliminated.

Pumpkin Seed Transporting Challenge

Each member of the team is given 15 seconds to transport pumpkin seeds from one bowl to another, using an iced tea spoon. Bowls are placed at opposite ends of the banquet table. Two teams may utilize the same table by having one team on each side and two bowls at each end.

Pumpkin Pie Feed

Blindfolded, the youngest member of each team feeds the oldest player on the team (also blindfolded) a piece of pumpkin pie. Remember, kids love whipped cream on their pie, so be sure to pile it on!

Featured Event

Pumpkin in the Straw

Hide candy and small prizes in loosely scattered straw. By age groups, allow children to come up and find treats. Play "Turkey in the Straw" in the background to enliven their efforts. Give each group one to two minutes to locate treats before "reseeding" the straw for the next age group. Once age groups have participated in this challenge, invite them to sit and watch the other groups.

Team Awards and Refreshments

Announce the winner of the "Guess the Number of Candies" contest. If you kept track of team scores, announce the standings of each team and give a small prize to members of the winning team. Suggested refreshments: orange juice, pumpkin-shaped cookies, pumpkin bread or muffins. Distribute goodie bags to participants as their parents arrive to pick them up.

A Salute to Cereal

Breakfast: the most important meal of the day. Of course, many of us skip it half the time, or we settle for coffee and a doughnut. Until now, breakfast has not gotten its just reward. Today, we honor breakfast, and the staple of that meal with (trumpet fanfare): A Salute to Cereal!

Atmosphere Enhancers

Try to create a mock up of a breakfast nook, with exaggerated features (e.g., jumbo clock and toaster, poster of cows, two-dimensional "kitchen cabinets" and a "refrigerator"). Cover tables with country kitchen tablecloths. Set out boxes of cereal, bowls, spoons, and washed, empty cartons of milk.

Getting Ready

- The area should be set up to allow for a large open playing space.

- Set up a registration table near the entrance. Check guests in and issue nametags. Be sure to print each name in large block letters for ease of reading.

- Set up a table for Guess the Number of Honeycombs game. Have someone count how many whole Honeycomb pieces it takes to fill a large cereal (or small serving) bowl. Cover the bowl with cellophane wrap to make sure you don't lose any of the game pieces! Set a tablet of paper and a pen on the table to record people's guesses. Make a large sign for the table: Guess the Number of Honeycombs in the Bowl!

- Purchase three boxes of different brands of the same type of cereal. Possibly use Cheerios, Corn Pops or Fruit Loops, and several store brand versions of the *same* cereal. Set up table and pour out cereal into tiny paper cups, making sure you keep track of which cereal is in which cups. Lay out enough cups of each cereal so most everyone can take a cup of each of the three cereals. Label each variety "A," "B," or "C." Place a piece of lined notebook paper and a pencil next to each label, and have the Cerealogist ask participants to write their name on the sheet of paper which corresponds to their cereal of preference.

- Assign someone to be the Cerealogist monitor for the Taste Test. Give this person a clipboard, paper, and pen. If more cups of cereal are needed, this person will need to (discreetly!) fill up more cups of cereal. Or, you may want to set out three large serving bowls, each with the different cereals, and place a stack of three-ounce paper cups in front of each. The Cerealogist may assist with distribution.

- Recruit someone to be Scorekeeper. Prepare posterboard with team names as headings. Have a marker available for adding and totaling scores during the program.

- Have an empty cereal bowl handy for Pass the Bowl.

- Prepare cups of cereal for Cereal Separators activity. Determine the number of teams you will want to have competing in your games. Each team will be given a decidedly different type of cereal. Honeycomb, Wheat Squares, Granola, Cheerios, or Cocoa Puffs might be good choices. Fill three-ounce paper cups approximately a third full with cereal of that team, filling enough cups for each participant to be given one. Fold the tops of the cups down so no one can see which type of cereal is inside.

- Set these cups on a tray in random arrangement. Make sure the tops of the cups are folded down to conceal the type of cereal that is in the cup.

- Tape the boxes from the cereal used for the Cereal Separators activity to the floor where you want the teams to line up for their team events.

- Ready a trash can with clean liner for each team for the Pound It Down game.

- Prepare props for Chex Mix Magic. Each team will need at least the following: three types of Chex cereal in one cup amounts (two cups of each type for a total of six cups of cereal per team), one quarter cup oil, two tablespoons Worcestershire Sauce, one teaspoon garlic powder, one teaspoon seasoned salt, and one half cup small pretzels—all placed in individual paper cups. If there will be more than 11 players per team, add more cups of cereal and/or pretzels. Keep each team's items separate.

- Have on hand a one-gallon or two-gallon reclosable storage bag per team.

- Make sure there is a microwave oven available for cooking the Chex Mix. After the Chex Mix Magic race, have an assistant microwave the bags according to package directions, place in a large bowl on the refreshments table.

- Purchase props for Dish It Out: an unopened box of Lucky Charms (one per team), a large (two-up size) cereal bowl for each team, and plastic spoons for each participant.

- Ready a plastic cereal bowl for each team, plus straight straws for each player.

- Have 6-foot to 8-foot banquet tables ready for use during Un-Lucky Charms. You will need one table for every two teams.

- Purchase several boxes of different brands of Raisin Bran, so each team has one box of approximately the same weight. Select both name and store brands for this event. Be prepared to put tables back out, and have a cereal bowl and a large mixing bowl ready for each team to use.

- Prepare props for the String You Along Team Challenge. Each team will need an unopened box of the same circle shaped cereal, such as Fruit Loops, Cracklin' Oat Bran, or Apple Jacks and a plastic darning needle, threaded with 12 feet of dental floss. Tie a button onto the end of each team's thread, to minimize frustration of slipping the cereal off the end.

- Assemble props for Breakfast Shooters: cereal bowl, water pistol filled with water (we'll call it clear milk), rain poncho, and two or three plastic grocery bags per team. You will also need a box or two of a "heavy" cereal, such as bite-sized wheat squares. This is a messy event! If this event will take place indoors, you will need to cover the playing area with plastic, and be prepared to clean up the inevitable mess!

- Have leadership team save nutrition label side bars from several different cereal boxes. Tape just the ingredients lists from these panels onto a sheet of paper. At the bottom of that sheet of paper, print the names of the cereals in random order. Photocopy these sheets so every team has one.

- Assemble appropriate prizes for Guess the Number of Honeycombs in the Bowl (a box of Honeycomb cereal), and for the winning team (individual serving size boxes).

- Prepare the refreshments table. Cover the table with "country" tablecloth. Set out the Chex Mix, Rice Krispies Treats, milk, cups, and napkins.

Group Starters

Guess the Number of Honeycombs

Encourage participants to make a guess as to how many honeycombs there are in the bowl. Have them write their name and their guess on the tablet of paper provided.

Taste Test

Set out little cups of several different varieties of the "same" cereal. Label them "A," "B," "C," and so on. Have a Cerealogist monitor this experiment, clipboard in hand. (Have this person wear a lab coat to make them look scientific!) Participants sample a few of each of the cereals, and rate them according to taste and/or texture preference. Tally the results, and announce the group's consensus at the end of the program.

Welcome

Ever notice how we often take for granted the things we love most? Instead of giving them due honor, we ignore them and the value they have for enriching our lives. Well, I say, "No more!" We are here today to pay tribute to a staple of life here in America. We can get puffed up with pride today. We aren't a bunch of flakes who have gathered for no raisin, I mean reason. Ladies and gentlemen, let us rise and pay tribute to the popular—no other food gets as much shelf space in a grocery store—yet humble source of 10 vitamins and minerals that gets you started in the morning and makes a great snack any time of the day.

Pass the Bowl

Gather the group in a circle. Beginning with the leader, pass an empty cereal bowl around the circle, person to person. Have each one state his or her name and favorite cereal before passing the bowl along.

Team Dividing

Cereal Separators

Explain to the group that this exercise will divide the group into teams. Name the teams, and point out the places on the floor where the front of the box of cereal has been taped down. When told to do so, teams should line up behind their cereal box. Place cups on a tray, and "serve" participants a cup. Participants should *not* unfold their cups of cereal until told to do so, once everyone is served. Once everyone has a cup, let players race to see which team can line themselves single-file behind their box first. (DO NOT let players eat their cereal—yet!)

Team Events

Pound It Down

Have players stand facing their cereal box. Place a trash can behind each team. On the "go" signal the first person in line "pounds down" the cereal, and passes the empty cup person-to-person down the line to the last person. That person throws the cup into the trash can, and races to the front of the line with his or her cup of cereal, careful to not spill it. When he or she gets to the front position, the person pops the cereal in his or her mouth, and sends the cup person-to-person down the line. Play continues until the first person has returned to the starting position.

Chex Mix Magic

Each team member gets an ingredient for making Chex mix. In turn, they race to their team leader, who stands 10 yards away with an open reclosable storage bag (one or two gallon size). Once all the ingredients have been put inside, the team leader zippers the bag shut, and shakes.

> **Leaders:** Take the bags of mixed up ingredients and microwave them according to package directions, for consumption later at the refreshments table.

Dish It Out

Hand the first player in each line a box of Lucky Charms, and the last player in each line a large cereal bowl (approximately two-cup size). Give each of the other players a plastic spoon. On the "go" signal, the first player in line opens the box. The second player scoops out a spoonful of cereal, and transfers the cereal to the next person's spoon. Once the person has emptied his or her spoonful, he may scoop another spoonful out of the box, and continue passing the cereal down the line, spoon to spoon. The last person in line continues to collect cereal in the bowl until the leader declares it full.

Un-Lucky Charms

Use the cereal bowl full of Lucky Charms from the last game. Place each team's cereal bowl on one end of a table, and an empty bowl on the other, approximately four feet away. Each player is given a plastic straw. Players take 20–30 second turns trying to eradicate the marshmallow pieces from the cereal, using a sucking action through their straws. Marshmallow pieces are transported via straw to a separate bowl, on the far end of the table.

Cereal Studies

Give each team a new, unopened box of Raisin Bran. Each box should be approximately the same weight package, but different brands. Use several national brands as well as local grocery chain varieties. On "go" teams race to separate out the raisins, and figure out which team/brand really has the most raisins. Now *this* is science!

Stringing You Along Team Challenge

The object of this event is to string a circle shaped cereal. On the "go" signal, hand each team an unopened box of cereal. (Have teams use the same sized box of the same type of cereal.) Teams race to see who can string their box of cereal first *and* make the longest strand of cereal.

Featured Event

Breakfast Shooters

One person per team volunteers to be the Breakfast Eater. He or she is given a rain poncho to wear, and has his or her shoes covered with plastic bags. The Breakfast Eater holds an empty cereal bowl. Team mates line up opposite this person, and try to fill the bowl by tossing cereal into it. (Heavier cereals, such as bite-size wheat squares are easier to toss than light ones.) Once the bowls are full, or have a predetermined number of morsels tossed in, give one teammate a water pistol full of "clear" milk (aka, water), and have her "shoot" moisture onto the cereal. The winning team is the one who empties its milk pistol first—providing there is a noticeable amount of milk in the bowl!

Cool Down

Ingredients Intrigue

While the leaders help get the Breakfast Eaters cleaned up, let the rest of their team move on to this cool down event. Hand each team a pencil and a sheet of paper which lists the ingredients from several varieties of breakfast cereals. Also included is a list of the cereals. Team mates work together to try to match the cereal name with its list of ingredients, within the time given (three minutes or so). Share answers with the group to determine how many each team guessed correctly. Award appropriate points for each correct answer.

Award Prizes

Reward the winner of the Guess the Number of Honeycombs game with (what else?) a box of Honeycomb cereal! Announce the best tasting cereal from your taste test. Award a prize for the winning team, too—perhaps individual serving, snack-size boxes of cereal.

Closing

There's no accounting for taste when it comes to our favorite cereals. Some of us like flaky cereals, others prefer the sugar-coated crunchy ones. That's OK! This is America. We can like different varieties, and still get along! The important thing is that we give due respect to this humble staple of life with "A Salute to Cereal!"

Refreshments

- Chex Mix (which the teams mixed and a leader microwaved during the program)
- Rice Krispies treats
- Milk

Supermarket Super Night

There's a lot of fun to be had at a grocery store, especially when you're a kid and you can race through the aisles! A comical combination of mental stimulation and shear physical exercise, Supermarket Super Night is a great program for the elementary/preadolescent crowd.

Getting Ready

- Well ahead of this event, begin saving empty boxes and cartons from cereal, frozen dinners, cake mixes, yogurt, orange juice, chips, and the like. Wash them out as necessary. Tape lids shut, after stuffing cartons with newspaper, if necessary to give shape to the container. Wash out cans, preserving the labels. With a strip of masking tape or duct tape, cover the sharp open edge of each can. Please do *not* use any glass jars for this event.

- Save the coupon sections of several Sunday newspapers.

- Locate four to six 8-foot banquet tables.

- Create labels for the tables to indicate types of products. (e.g., Cereals, Baking Products, Canned Vegetables, Dairy, Frozen Foods).

- Set up registration table with sign-in sheets and nametags.

- Set a few grocery items on a table with a sheet of paper and pencil. Make a placard inviting participants to write their names on the paper and their guess as to the actual retail price of the items on the table. You may have them guess each item separately or collectively. Items might include a loaf of bread, a jar of peanut butter, and a jar of jelly; or a can of soup and a box of crackers.

- Secure a prize for the winner of the guess the price challenge.

- Set out a table with coupon inserts from newspapers and several pairs of scissors.

- Set up a table for paper bags, markers, and crayons.

- Designate someone to monitor and give directions at the paper bag table.

- Recruit a Candy Meister.

- Designate an area for participants to place their paper bags, arranged by grade level. The Candy Meister will assign teams by selecting players for each team from each grade. This should make for somewhat equal teams.

- Provide pencil and paper for the Candy Meister to write down team names and members.

- In the main event area, set up a circle of chairs for seating each participant and all leaders.

- Secure several plastic grocery baskets for Musical Baskets.

- Ask a store for a strip of 20 "paid" stickers, or use another type of sticker or hand stamp for the Pass the Basket game.

- For each team, prepare a box or sack of groceries. Each team should have the same number of items in their box, probably twice as many items as there are players on the team.

- Locate 12 rolls of individually wrapped toilet paper for each team.

- Purchase enough snack-size raisin boxes for each participant to have one. Allow for a few extras.

- Borrow enough push brooms for each team to have one.

- Have double-bagged large paper grocery bags ready for each team. (They need to be strong!)

- Prepare a list of groceries for each team to collect from the tables. Each list should contain the same number of items.

- Small prizes needed for grocery baggers (one person per team), and for players recognized as "excellent employees."

- On a large sheet of paper or posterboard, write "Exemplary Employee Wall of Fame." Have several markers for these "employees" to write their names on the paper.

- Prepare cartons/packages for closing story.

Registration and Nametags

Welcome each young guest personally, and write the child's name in large block letters on the name tag. On the corner write the number of what grade the child is in (e.g., K, 1, 2, 3).

Group Starters

Total It Up

Guess the price of the different grocery items on the table. Children look at the grouping of groceries you have set out. Have each one guess how much money it would cost to purchase those items at the grocery store.

Personalize Your Parcel

Decorate paper bags (including the child's name and grade). Have children give their candy bags to the Candy Meister, who groups them according to grade.

Welcome

Name Pass

Pass a grocery basket from person to person. Have each person say his name and an item he would like to put into the basket from a grocery store.

Mixers

Supermarket Shuffle

The leader reads aloud these grocery items: milk, bread, eggs, cereal, juice. Each person silently chooses one of the given items. One of the leaders stands in middle of circle. (Her chair has been removed, so there are no extra chairs.) This person calls out the name of one of the items from the list. Everyone who has selected that item must stand up and move to a different chair. "It" tries to occupy a temporarily vacant seat. Whoever is left standing is "it" for the next round. "It" may chose to call "Supermarket Shuffle!" On that command, *everyone* must stand up and change chairs.

Musical Baskets

Start several baskets around the circle at different starting points. When the music stops, whoever is holding the basket gets a "paid" sticker, which may be cashed in at the end for an extra piece of candy. Play this several times.

Team Games

Orientation of New Employees

Explain to "employees" our grocery store's motto: We value a neat, clean appearance in our store, and a cooperative, friendly attitude in our staff. Show participants the gold stars which may be periodically awarded to staff members who prove to be exemplary employees. Watch for youngsters who make an effort to behave, play fairly, or encourage other players. Award gold stars and have children place them on their nametags. Players with these gold stars should receive an extra little prize at the end of the event, and should write their names on the Wall of Fame.

Stocking Shelves

Have tables set up with labels of where each type of grocery item belongs.) Each team is given a box or sack of groceries. On "go," teams shelve items, one per person, one at a time, taking care they are shelved properly and neatly.

High Stacking

Each team is given 12 rolls of individually wrapped toilet paper rolls. One person, one roll at a time runs up and adds a roll to the stack, seeing which team can get theirs up and standing first, and as high as possible. If the stack tumbles down, the player may reassemble the stack.

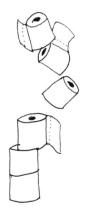

Domino Boxes

Each player on each team is given a snack-size box of raisins. In turn, players run to table, and set their box an inch behind the previous one, along the facing edge of the table (so we can watch). After each player has placed her box, the first person runs back up and taps the first box (the one he placed there), knocking over the whole row. The first team to complete the sequence wins!

Restacking Domino Boxes

Each player runs back up, retrieves a box, sets it up at the opposite end of table.

Sweeping Aisles Relay

Each team gets a push broom. In turn, each player sweeps up the right side of their table, and down the left, handing off the broom to the next racer. First team to make a clean sweep wins.

Bagging Groceries Instruction

Each team sends a representative to receive instruction in "proper" bagging. Following instruction, the representatives will load a bag with grocery items. Representatives receive a sticker, which can be redeemed later for a prize. This is not a speed event.

Bag Carrying Relay

Using the just-bagged groceries, each team member takes the bag, runs it around their table, and passes it to the next person, until each player has had a turn carrying the groceries.

Restock Groceries

Again, one item at a time, one person at a time, everything gets reshelved.

Featured Activity

Speed Shopping

Each coach is given a grocery list and a shopping basket. On "go" the first player is told what one item to retrieve, and given the shopping basket to go and get it, then return, handing the basket to the next player. The coach then tells the next person what the next item is to be retrieved.

Cool Down

Picking Favorites

On a table in front of the participants, several delectable treat boxes/cartons are displayed. Ask the kids, "What looks good to you?" Open each package they indicate, and see what is inside. Place things like plastic bugs or moldy cheese in the fancier, more desirable boxes. In the "least desirable" package, place an object most children would like, such as a bean bag animal, cool markers, or something that would be perceived by the group as desirable.

> **Lesson:** Appearances can be beautiful and/or intriguing, but it is what is inside, the character of a person, that matters. Be more concerned with the heart or character of a person than the external features or appearance.

Award Prizes

Recognize excellent employees with treats or prizes. Congratulate all employees on a fine evening's work and thank them all for their efforts in helping you achieve your store's mission. Distribute goodie bags to all participants and prizes to the winning team. If desired, distribute a snack for participants to enjoy while waiting for parents to arrive.

This Spud's for You

A Plethora of Potato Fun for the Whole Family!

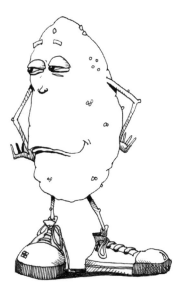

This is the ultimate in playing with your food! We will grab potatoes, toss potatoes, sweep potatoes, shape potatoes, even squish potatoes between our toes! This is not a program for the faint of heart. Rather, this event has been designed as a starch sensation, a tuber triumph, a tater elater, a spud spectacular! If you like potatoes in any form, This Spud's for You!

Atmosphere Enhancers

Transform your play area into a County Fair. Bluegrass music can be played in the background and leaders should wear lots of denim, bandanas, and straw hats. Decorate with items such as the following:

- 50-pound bag of potatoes (also use for a guess the number of potatoes in the sack contest).

- pitchfork or hoe.

- bales of straw.

- scarecrow.

- wagon or farm implements.

- posters from Idaho (about potatoes).

- boxes or bags of potato products (made to look full).

- red and white checkered tablecloths.

Getting Ready

- Set up a registration table near the entrance to your play area.

- Lay out nametags and markers. Ask participants to write their names in large block letters so they are easy to read.

- Set up Individual Tater Tot Toss group starter game. Purchase a large bag of frozen Tater Tots and locate at least four nonglass bowls of various sizes. Label them Catsup, Honey, Dijon, and BBQ Sauce, and give them each a different point value (e.g., 10, 20, 30, and 50 points). Have tokens available for players who score at least 100 points with their five Tater Tots.

- Purchase 1-ounce bags of potato chips to give as prizes for Individual Tater Toss.

- Cover two large tables with plastic for Spud Sculptures. Mix some *thick* instant mashed potatoes, about two to four cups per artist. Distribute paper plates or clean, foam meat trays, (plastic) butter knives, forks, and other texture producing tools. (Have a wash basin and towels handy, too!) If desired, add food coloring to some of the piles of potato "clay." (Blend well before distributing.)

- Recruit judges for Spud Sculptures, and have prizes for category winners.

- Recruit someone to serve as Scorekeeper for the team events.

- Recruit someone to be in charge of the Spud Bowl Trivia Challenge. This person should review the questions and answers, and be able to "jump in" when there is a lull between activities.

- Create a scoreboard, and label with the team names. Have a marker available for the Scorekeeper to use.

- Locate the largest potato you can, purchase it and record the weight to the nearest 100th of a pound. "Dress" potato like a superhero, and make a sign that says, "Guess the Weight of Super Spud." Have participants record their guesses.

- Acquire a 50-pound sack of potatoes, any variety or size. Count the number of potatoes in the sack (and write that number down somewhere!) Make a sign that reads, "Guess the number of potatoes in the sack!" Have paper and pen ready for contestants to write their name and guess.

- Locate a Mr. Potato Head for passing at the initial introductions activity.

- Set up a CD player or PA system that will broadcast music. Have some bluegrass music playing in the background as people arrive and mingle. You will also need some lively music playing during the games. See games explanations for suggested songs.

- Purchase sheets of color paper in as many different colors as you will have teams. Also purchase a large sheet of manila or white newsprint paper. From the color and white papers, create the following pieces, so each team will have a complete set in their particular team color: two eyes, two eyebrows, a nose, a mouth, two ears, a hat, a mustache, a bow tie, and a large "potato head." You may, of course, use different colors for accents, but it should be obvious which is the primary color for each piece. The pieces should be "jumbo-sized." The eyes, for instance, should be about the size of a CD. If you will have more or fewer than 12 players per team, adjust the number of facial features and accessories accordingly.

- Have masking tape ready for fastening the pieces to Mr. Potato Head.

- Acquire enough plain, large, paper grocery bags for each team to have one, plus allow for a few extras.

- Get a bale of straw. Also get enough small potatoes for each participant to have one.

- If possible, secure a large, fabric potato sack for each team. Otherwise, locate an old blanket for each team to use for dragging a teammate around a slalom course.

- Secure a cooking pot for each team, for collecting potatoes.

- Assemble props for the Shoot Out at the Ore-Ida Corral. Each team will need a cowboy hat, bandana, a cup of water, two "holsters" filled with three to six French fries each (depending on the size of the contestant), a means for fastening the holsters to the contestant (e.g., metal binder clips from any stationary department of a retail store to attach to waistband, or a piece of rope that could be tied around the waist). If you do not have access to toy cowboy holsters, ask a fast food chain to let you have some of their large cardboard fry containers to use.

- Recruit an assistant to warm up the fries just prior to this activity. (Cold fries taste nasty!)

- Assign leaders to monitor this speed eating event, watching for possible choking incidents. This person should have a supply of paper towels on hand, and cups of water for contestants to drink.

- Purchase a bottle of catsup as a prize for the winner the of fry eating contest.

- Review the suggested featured activities (p. 154) to determine which, if either, you would like to conduct. Secure the necessary supplies. Be sure to do a practice run with your leadership team!

- Prepare prizes for the winning team, Guess the Number of Potatoes, and Guess the Weight of Super Spud.

Registration Table

Have participants sign in as they arrive, and write their names on nametags. Invite the guests to participate in the Group Starter activities, which should already be laid out.

Group Starters

I have included many group starters for this event—there are so many ways to have fun with potatoes! You can use all of them, allowing extra time for participants to get to try each activity. Or, if you prefer, you can select just a few of these to get the group started on some terrific tater times!

Individual Tater Tot Toss

As participants arrive, they are given five Tater Tots which they try to toss into bowls marked with different point values. (Perhaps have each bowl labeled Catsup, Honey, Dijon, and BBQ Sauce.) Players scoring more than a certain number win a prize—like a one-ounce bag of chips—or they can be given a "Tater Token" which can be redeemed at the end of the program for a prize.

Guess the Number of Potatoes

Prop the sack up next to a "guess the number" sign, place a sheet of paper for guesses next to it, and you're ready to go. (Of course you'll need to count how many potatoes there are before participants arrive!)

Spud Sculptures

Mix up some *thick* instant mashed potatoes (one cup flakes to one half cup water). Allow about two to four cups per artist. Distribute paper plates or clean, foam meat trays, (plastic) knives, forks, and other texture producing tools. (Have a wash basin and towels handy, too.) If desired, add food coloring to some of the piles of potato "clay." Blend well before distributing.

Give contestants 10 to 15 minutes to create their masterpieces, then display and judge them. You may want to suggest topics, or have judging categories: best likeness of someone in the room, most intricate, most creative use of potatoes, best replica of a famous landmark...

Guess the Weight of Super Spud

Go to the store or local farmer's market and purchase the largest potato you can find. Record its weight, down to the nearest 100th of a pound. Display Super Spud on game night (perhaps adorned with a cape, to accentuate its super powers), and have participants guess its weight.

Mixers

Start off your program with a welcome to the group and an opportunity for each person to share his or her name. Pass a Mr. Potato Head, allowing each person to state his name (loudly!) as the creature is passed along to the next participant or leader.

Team Dividing

Distribute Mr. Potato Head paper pieces you prepared. Explain what each piece is—eye, ear, mouth, nose, eyebrow, etc. Also show on each piece where the color is that will determine teams. For example, the Blue team would be comprised of those players who have blue on the jumbo-sized eyes, eyebrows, nose, mouth, ears, hat, mustache, bow tie, and potato head. This game leads into the next.

Select appropriate potato team names, such as Order of Fries, Smashed Potatoes, The Baked Bunch, Tater Tots, Idaho Burbank Russets, or Ruffles With Ridges. Each team should be assigned a corresponding color.

Relays and Team Events

Mr. Potato Head Relay

Once the teams have been determined by the color of the Mr. Potato Head pieces, they form a relay line, and are issued strips of masking tape. In turn, the leader explains, players race up in turn and decorate Mr. Potato Head, Once everyone is set with those directions, have the players holding the potato head piece come up and get paper bags placed over their heads—they will be the Mr. or Ms. Potato Heads! Play some lively music in the background to add to the excitement.

Potato Bowl

Use some of the questions from the Spud Bowl Trivia Challenge as needed as a filler between activities (see pp. 152–155).

Tater In A Haystack (Or) Digging Fer Taters

Open and scatter a bale of straw in one corner of your game area. Mix in some *small* potatoes, burying many of them. Team players take turns running up, digging out a tater, and returning. Play "Turkey in the Straw" or a similar song as background music.

Potato Sack Slalom

Players keep a hold of the potato they just collected. Each team selects one player to "do" the slalom course (someone small), and one player to pull the small player. Other team members line up, spacing themselves approximately six to eight feet apart. On "go" the pulling player grabs hold of the potato sack the other player is sitting on, and pulls him around the slalom course, weaving in and out around the other team players. As the pair progresses, teammates gently deposit their potatoes in a pot that the rider is holding. Guard against players getting slingshot off course and into the ionosphere! The first team to successfully complete the course, having gathered all their team's potatoes wins.

Shoot Out At The Ore-Ida Corral

Each team selects their best hope for winning this French fry eating contest. When contestants are chosen, they come to a central spot in the playing area. Each is issued a cowboy hat, a neck bandana, and two "holsters" filled with fries (about three to six fries per holster). Ask a fast food chain to give you empty, large fry containers, two per team. Use metal binder clips to fasten holsters to the waistband of contestants' pants or shorts. Contestants begin by standing back to back in the center of the playing area. When instructed to do so, players advance three steps, then spin around and begin scarfing down their fries. The first contestant to eat all her fries and yell, "Finished Fries First"—with an empty mouth—wins honor, glory, prestige, and a bottle of catsup! (You may want to substitute some other fabulous prize for the catsup.) Let the person monitoring this game distribute cups of water to the contestants, to wash down the fries.

Featured Activities

You have your choice of either of the two styles of potatoes listed below. Review both options to determine which goes better with your group. Would you like that with sour cream and butter?

Spud Walk

Fill an aluminum turkey roasting pan (or kiddy wading pool) with three to four inches of thin mashed potatoes. If indoors, place the roasting pan (pool) in the center of a vinyl tablecloth or plastic drop cloth, allowing at least two to three feet of cloth extending beyond the pan. Have a plastic tub of water, and plenty of towels available for washing off legs and feet. In the tub, place three dozen marbles or pebbles. (These are the "eyes.") Have competitions to see who can remove the most potato eyes in a given amount of time. Depending on the size of the pool, you may run individual competitions, or two-on-two challenges, or even tag team competitions.

Potato Ball Fights

The perfect outdoor option for a featured event! It may be too hot out for a snowball fight, but with the amazing new "Potato Ball" you can enjoy the excitement of winter in the comfortable temperatures of summer!

Mix up some "thin" mashed potatoes, divide the group into two teams, and let them fling the "Potato Slush" at one another! "Normal" ratio is one cup flakes to one cup water. Start with a thinner mixture, so it barely holds a ball shape. Sloppy spuds make a great splat! Once the mixture gets thick enough to form a good "snow ball" it is hard enough to hurt someone, which spoils the game for the victim. Let the fun be in the flurry of flinging slurry, rather than in serious stings of missiles. When all the ammo is used up, give the kids (and the field!) a good hosing down!

Cool Down

Spud Bowl Trivia Challenge

Your Potato Trivia Expert probably asked the group many of these questions during breaks between games. Any remaining questions should be asked now (see pp. 152–155).

Award Prizes

As you wrap up this spud-tacular event, have your Spud Judges announce the winners of Guess the Number of Spuds and Guess the Weight of Super Spud. Also have them display winning Spud Sculptures and what was particularly award-winning about each. Team standings should also be announced and prizes given. Be sure to thank both the participants and the leadership team for their efforts and attendance.

Refreshments

Consider the time of day you will be holding this event to best determine appropriate refreshments.

- Potato chips
- Potato pancakes
- French fries
- Potato soup
- Tater Tots
- Potato chip cookies

Spud Bowl Trivia Challenge

Spud Joke to get things started:

Q: Why didn't the mother want her daughter to marry the famous TV newscaster?

A: Because he was just a common tater.

True Or False Questions

All answers are TRUE

1. Potatoes come in red, white, blue, and yellow.

2. The "seedballs" of the potato plant are poisonous.

3. The "Irish" white potato we are most familiar with today originally came from the Andes of South America.

4. The Incas of South America freeze dried potatoes. This freeze dried "chuno" would keep for four years.

5. Inca Indians based some of their units of time on how long it took for a potato to cook.

6. The Irish potato famine of 1845–1846 killed over 1,000,000 people.

7. Some potatoes have purple flesh.

8. The sweet potato belongs to the same family as the morning glory, while the white potato belongs to the same family as tomatoes, tobacco, chile pepper, eggplant, and petunia.

9. The world's largest potato chip was produced by the Pringles Company and was 23-inches by 14.5-inches.

10. Mr. Potato Head gave up his pipe and became the unofficial "spokespud" of the American Cancer Society Great American Smokeout in 1987.

11. The most potatoes grown on a single plant weighed 370 pounds.

12. The biggest potato ever grown was 7 pounds 1 ounce.

13. (Save if needed) The _____ is a variety of potato grown in the United States.

True	False
Belrus	Slimer
Green Mountain	Dennis Perry
Irish Cobbler	Dolly Parton
Shepody	Golden Delicious
Carola	Texas Pete
Goldrush	Vineyard Special
Kennebec	Sweet Ambrosia
Yukon Gold	Old Grandad
Katahdin	Depth Charger

Multiple Guess Questions

14. One of the following is considered to be nearly a perfect food. In fact, according to the U.S. Department of Agriculture, a diet of whole milk and this food "would supply almost all of the food elements necessary for the maintenance of the human body." Which is this wonderful food?
    A. **Potatoes**
    B. Pop Tarts
    C. Snickers bars
    D. Lightning bugs

15. One medium potato has about how many calories?
    A. 10
    B. **110**
    C. 350
    D. 1,000

16. The average American eats how many pounds of potatoes each year?
    A. 10
    B. 50
    C. **124**
    D. 250

17. The Idaho Potato Exposition, located in Blackfoot, Idaho, is the self-proclaimed "Potato Capital of the World." Which of the following will you NOT find at the Idaho Potato Expo?

A. A fabulous potato harvest diorama
B. Potato fudge
C. A kitchen which offers "Free Taters for Out of Staters."
D. The largest potato chip in the world
E. **You will find ALL of the above at the Idaho Potato Expo**

18. Spanish explorers introduced potatoes to Europe in which century?
A. **16th**
B. 17th
C. 18th
D. 19th

19. Potatoes did not become popular in Europe until which of the following famous people paraded through the French countryside with potato blossoms in her hair?
A. Cleopatra
B. Lady Godiva
C. Joan of Arc
D. **Marie Antoinette**

20. When was Mr. Potato Head first introduced?
A. 1929
B. 1946
C. **1952**
D. 1961

21. How many varieties of potatoes are there in the world?
A. 5
B. 50
C. 500
D. **5,000**

22. Which of the following is a variety of potato grown in the United States?
A. Spectacular Sarver
B. Magnificent Martin
C. Powerful Pond
D. **Irish Cobbler**

23. A potato is about 80% _____.
A. **Water**
B. Starch

C. Fiber
D. Dirt

24. The first president to serve French fries at the White House was:
A. Ronald McDonald
B. Abraham Lincoln
C. **Thomas Jefferson**
D. William Taft

25. Potatoes grow commercially in how many of the 50 U.S. states?
A. 1
B. 3
C. 15
D. **50**

26. The most nutrients in a potato are found in and around the:
A. Center
B. Juice
C. **Skin**
D. Discarded grease from McDonalds' french fryers

27. The number one state for producing potatoes is:
A. Alaska
B. **Idaho**
C. Hawaii
D. New Jersey

28. The average American eats approximately how many pounds of french fries each year?
A. 25
B. 15
C. **60**

29. The average American eats how many pounds of potato chips each year?
A. 23
B. 198
C. **17**

30. The average American eats how many pounds of fresh potatoes each year?
A. 100
B. **50**
C. 140

This Spud's for You 2

If the Spud Fits, Wear It!

The National Potato Council is right—potatoes are a versatile vegetable! We had so many incredible ideas for playing with potatoes, we created a second fabulous food fest focusing on this often overlooked oval. Feel free to mix and match the activities from both spud events. Spuds—they're not just for eating anymore!

Getting Ready

- Set up a registration table near the entrance to your play area.

- Lay out nametags and markers. Make sure you ask participants to write their names in large block letters, so they are easy to read.

- On a banquet table, lay out several bowls with different brands of potato chips. Mark each bowl—A, B, C, and so on. In front of each bowl set a piece of paper and a pen. Label the table: Taste Test! Vote for the best tasting chip. Be sure to hide the potato chip bags so contestants don't know what they are eating. Select several national brands as well as some store brands and baked potato chip varieties.

- Prepare the Potato Decorating table. Have enough potatoes on hand for each person to have one to decorate. Set out materials to create Mr. or Mrs. Potato Heads, including craft pins with large heads, scissors, pieces of color felt, posterboard for feet, foam sheets and markers, and patterns/illustrations of different style mouths, noses, eyes, ears, and eyebrows.

- Recruit several people to be judges for the decorated potatoes. Come up with several categories (e.g., most bizarre, most colorful, prettiest, most like someone we know...) Be sure to have a small prize to present as well, perhaps a Mr. Potato Head keychain.

- Set up Longest Potato Peel station. On a covered six-foot banquet table, place a dozen or more potatoes, several potato peelers, a stack of cheap paper plates and a pen or permanent marker. Make a label that says, "Longest Potato Peel." Set out another label that says, "Please Use Caution: Peelers Are Sharp!"

- Purchase a three-pound bag of frozen french fries or get a fast food chain to donate several large orders of fries. Count the total number of fries and place them in a basket or container for viewing. Set out a tablet of paper and a pen for participants to record their names and guesses. You will need to use these same fries for the French Fry Phonics game later. If using frozen fries, have a freezer on hand for storing them after participants guess how many there are, to firm them back up before you use them for the spelling game.

- Recruit someone to serve as Scorekeeper for this event.

- Create a scoreboard, and label with the team names. Have a marker available for the Scorekeeper to use.

- Set out chairs so each player will have one. Chairs should be lined up to form a polygon of as many sides as you will have teams. Leave a little space on the end of each row for people to move between teams. If necessary, arrange each team's chairs to form two rows on their side of the polygon. Make sure you are able to move tables and props in and out to the center of the polygon by way of the corners.

- Acquire and wash enough potatoes to have one potato for every five players.

- Set up a CD player or PA system that can broadcast some lively bluegrass music during the Hot Potato game, and during other relays.

- Purchase jelly beans of as many different colors as you would like teams. There should be as many jelly beans of each color as there will be members of each team. Allow for a few extras of each color, just because they are tasty! Mix the colors together, and pour into several paper cups for your leadership team to distribute at the team dividing segment.

- Purchase a 20-ounce bag of frozen Tater Tots for each team. Store them in the freezer until the beginning of your event. If they are left out too long, they will be mushy. They should thaw rather quickly, but guard against overly energetic players who may be tempted to bean someone on the head with a solid, frozen missile.

- Secure enough large, metal or plastic mixing bowls for each team to use one. Also secure for each team an apron, a chef's hat, an oven mitt, and a pancake turner.

- Prepare a list of words and phrases to use in the French Fry Phonics game.

- Have several tables ready to move into position for French Fry Phonics.

- Bake as many large potatoes as you have teams, plus one extra for demonstration purposes.

- Locate six-foot to eight-foot long banquet tables for the Build a Better Baked Potato Relay. The more teams you have, the more tables you will need to hold the condiments. Use the same tables as for French Fry Phonics. Two or three teams could share the same table.

- Cover each table with a vinyl cloth. Set a tray on each table with the following items: a bowl of bacon bits, a squeeze bottle of margarine, a shaker of salt, a shaker of pepper, a container of sour cream, a bowl of chopped chives, a bowl of shredded cheese, a bowl of chopped broccoli, an aerosol can of whipped cream, a bowl of maraschino cherries, and plastic spoons for dipping ingredients out of the bowls. Additionally, each team will need a large, whole baked potato, a 12-inch square of aluminum foil, and a plastic butter knife.

- Have several banquet tables available for the Couples Mashed Potato Moment. You will need chairs to place along the sides, so each team can seat a couple on opposite sides of the table from one another. Expect to seat two to three couples per table.

- Assign someone to whip up some mashed potatoes prior to this event, so each team has a plastic cereal bowl full of warm smashed spuds. Each team will also need a large plastic serving spoon, a blindfold, a stack of paper towels or napkins, and a cup of water available to wash down the mashed potatoes after the event.

- Ready props for the Potato Mash event. Each team will need a vinyl tablecloth or sheet of plastic for under the chair of the participant who will be mixing the mashed potatoes, a turkey-size aluminum roasting pan or plastic tub, a large mixing bowl or plastic tub full of dry instant mashed potato flakes (approximately 10 cups per team), six 5-ounce plastic cups, a large, nonbreakable pitcher of water. If running this event outdoors, have a hose and water available for clean-up. If indoors, have plenty of old bath towels available.

- Secure prizes for winning team, Couples Mashed Potato Moment, and Potato People award winners.

Group Starters

Taste Testing Of Potato Chips

Set out several bowls of different brands of potato chips. Include several national brands, a store brand or two, and a variety of baked potato chips. Label each bowl A, B, C, etc., and place a sheet of paper with a corresponding label in front of each bowl. Set out several pencils or pens so participants can print their name on the sheet of paper which indicates their favorite chip. (At the end of the program, have someone announce what each type of chip was, and which got the most "votes" for best tasting chip.)

Potato Decorating

Each person gets a potato and decorates it Mr. Potato Head style with the materials provided.

Longest Potato Peel

While participants are still arriving, challenge guests to see how long a peel they can make using an ordinary potato peeler. Place each en-

try in the contest on a sheet of paper, and write the contestant's name on the paper. *Please* use caution with the peelers. They are sharp!

Guess The Number Of French Fries

Buy a three-pound bag of frozen french fries, or get several jumbo orders donated by a fast food restaurant. Count them, and display in an extra large basket, or use several large fries containers from a fast food restaurant.

When the game portion of the welcomes and introductions begins, have someone put the frozen fries back in the freezer for use in the French Fry Phonics game later in the program.

Welcome and Introductions

Potato Pass

Have the group form a circle. Give one person a potato. Have them yell out their first name and pass the potato to the next person. Everyone gets a feel for the group—and for the potato!

Musical Hot Potato

Distribute enough potatoes so every fifth player has a potato. Have players pass the potatoes to the person to their left, while the music plays. ("The Mashed Potato" would be an appropriate selection, or some lively bluegrass tune.) When the music is interrupted, players holding a potato form an outer circle, and the inner (original) circle tightens. Redistribute the potatoes, and continue with the next round. Continue playing until only a few players remain. As the number of players dwindles, so should the number of potatoes being passed. If desired, play until one player remains. Award the remaining player(s) a Tater Token, to be redeemed for a fabulous prize at the end of the program. (Maybe a gift certificate from Wendy's for, you guessed it, a baked potato.)

Team Dividing

While the group is standing in a circle around the final contestants of the Hot Potato event, have members of the leadership team distribute "mini sweet potatos" (aka, jelly beans) of as many different colors as you would like teams. Once every participant has received one, instruct the group to line up by color at a predetermined area. Chairs should be set up to form a polygon of as many sides as you will have teams. Each player should have a chair.

Team Events

Team Tater Tot Toss

Each team is given a bag of Tater Tots. Distribute them among team members. One team member stands in the center of the polygon playing area, opposite their group. Outfit each volunteer so he is wearing an apron, chef's hat, and oven mitt and holding a medium sized mixing bowl in one hand and a pancake turner in the other. On the "go" signal, each team tries to get as many Tater Tots as possible into the mixing bowl within 45 seconds. The pancake turner may be used to help keep Tots from bouncing out of the bowl. The time limitation adds to the franticness of the event. Each chef counts the number of Tater Tots in the mixing bowl at the end of the contest. Award 10 to 100 points (potato chips) for each Tater Tot in the bowl.

French Fry Phonics

Each team has a designated table (or space on a shared table) set up 15 feet from the front of their line, in the center of the polygon playing area. Each player is given three to five french fries. The leader calls out a word. If it is a three-letter word, the first three players on each team race to the table, and try to be the first group to spell out the word using their french fries. Potato Chips (points) are awarded to the first team do spell the word correctly and legibly. Those

players return to the back of the line, and everyone else moves forward. Round two begins when the next spelling word is given. Words should get progressively longer and more difficult.

Build a Better Baked Potato Relay

Baked potatoes are a favorite for many people. The toughest decision at a baked potato bar is deciding what toppings to put on your spud. We've eliminated that source of stress in your life in this next relay: Your team puts a little of everything on it! Assemble teams relay style, facing a table, approximately 30 feet away. Stock the table with the following: one baked potato per team, one 12-inch square of aluminum foil per team, a jar of bacon bits, a squeeze bottle of margarine, shakers of salt and pepper, a container of sour cream, a bowl of chopped chives, a bowl of shredded cheese, a bowl of chopped broccoli, an aerosol can of whipped cream, a bowl of maraschino cherries, plastic spoons for dipping ingredients out of the bowls, a plastic knife for each team, and serving spoons in the appropriate containers.

On the "go" signal, the first person from each team races up to the table, grabs a large baked potato, and races back to the team, handing the spud off to the next player. This player runs to the table, grabs a square of aluminum foil, and wraps the potato, leaving one of the sides exposed. (Basically, she has made an aluminum foil "bowl" for the potato.) She then returns to her team, and hands the baked spud off to the next player. This player races to the table, carefully selects a plastic knife, and makes one long incision in the potato, and one short crossways incision. By grasping the two pointy ends of the potato and pushing toward the middle of the potato, then out again, players can make a decent cavity for filling with toppings. The rest of the race involves teammates racing back and forth in turn, adding different toppings to the potato. The last two players should put on the aerosol whipped cream and maraschino cherry, respectively. Judges determine the fastest team to successfully top their tater. Toppings must remain on the potato to count!

Couples Mashed Potato Moment

A contest for those not of faint heart—or stomach! Each team selects a couple to represent them. Each couple decides which one of them enjoys mashed potatoes the most. That person becomes known as the Eater. The other partner becomes the Feeder. Couples from all the teams stand around a centrally located table, Eaters on one side, Feeders on the other. The game is simple enough. Each couple will get a bowl of warm mashed potatoes, which the Feeder feeds to the Eater. Add a few slight complications: the Eater must place (and keep) her hands behind her back, while the blindfolded Feeder uses a large serving spoon to feed his partner! Bon Apetite!

Featured Activity

Potato Mash

Mix up a batch of mashed potatoes—using your feet. Have each team sit side by side with their own teammates. At one end of the line, place a large bowl full of instant mashed potato flakes, six 5-ounce plastic cups, and a large nonbreakable pitcher of water. The person at the other end of the line should sit on a chair. (It would be wise to cover the chair with a large trash can liner or sheet of vinyl.) The contestant on the chair should remove her shoes, roll up her pant legs, and place her bare feet in a large pan. (A turkey size aluminum roasting pan or large plastic storage tub would work well.) If you are running this relay indoors, be sure to spread a plastic tarp under each end player's area! If you are outdoors, have a hose ready for cleanup.

On the "go" command, the first player in each line fills a five-ounce cup with potato flakes and passes it to the second person in line. While this cup makes its way person to person down the line to the next-to-the-end player to dump into their team's pan, the lead player fills another cup, and begins passing it along. Full cups of mashed potato flakes continue making their way down the line, person to person, while empty cups are relayed back in a similar fashion. When all the potato flakes have been passed, the lead player then begins filling the cups with water, and sends them down the "conveyer belt" of people. As soon as a few cups full of water have been passed, the person sitting at the far end of the team's

line begins working the water into the flakes—with her bare feet. When the mixture is the consistency of, well, mashed potatoes, the team yells out, 'We've got mashed potatoes!" Judges should be monitoring each team's progress, and will determine which team finished in winning order. Make sure you've got plenty of old towels on hand for those with mashed potato-toes!

Cool Down

Awards

Take this opportunity to award the winner of "Guess the Number of Fries" and present a suitable prize—something "potato-y."

Bring out the "Potato People" that participants created at the onset of the event. Present awards for the "Best" ones for each category you selected. A Mr. Potato Head key chain or poster would be great prizes. Heck, even a five-pound bag of the tubers themselves would be great—something winners would cherish for many meals to come!

You may want to present the end players from the last game with a little prize for their efforts, too. Calculate team scores and award an appropriate potato-related prize to members of the winning team.

Be sure to acknowledge your leadership team and thank them for their assistance. Thank the group for making the event so much fun, and personally thank as many participants for coming as possible. Then move on to potato-y refreshments!

Turkey Time

If you're looking for a spirited Thanksgiving program for younger kids, look no further! Turkey Time is the perfect program for you. The kids will enjoy the relays, races, and cute turkey theme. You'll enjoy watching them have so much fun!

Getting Ready

- Prepare nametags for participants, with animal symbols on them to distinguish teams.

- Set up table with paper and pencil for Guess the Number of Mini Turkey Eggs (aka, malt balls or jellybeans) in the jar. Ready jar as well, by counting and recording the exact number of candies.

- Collect materials for hand cutouts: construction paper of different colors, markers or crayons for writing names, pencils for outlining hands, scissors for cutting out paper hands. Set them out on a table along with a finished example.

- Locate several (one per team) plastic drumsticks, as from a child's toy cooking set. Mark each one with a separate color to distinguish teams.

- Set up boom box for Musical Drumsticks.

- Recruit someone to act as Scorekeeper and supply him or her with paper and pencil.

- Locate as many cobs of Indian or field corn as you will have teams.

- Prepare "feed buckets" with whole, shell-on peanuts, so each team has a bucket, and each player gets at least five peanuts. Also ready a large shoebox per team.

- For each team, create a cardboard turkey beak with elastic band and a belt with tail feathers attached.

- Draw a turkey on a piece of posterboard. Mark an "X" near its tail. Laminate, or cover with clear Contact brand paper.

- From construction paper, cut out enough "feathers" for each player to have two. Make a few extras. Attach half of them (one per player) to the laminated turkey using masking tape, and hang poster on wall. Keep extra masking tape available.

- Ready blindfolds (one per team).

- Locate a large trash can liner, brown, if possible. Cut two leg holes in the bottom. Have a good supply of newspaper on hand for stuffing the liner, and have duct tape available for holding the liner in place. Bring an old shirt for the "Turkey" to wear, one which can tolerate being duct taped. Use a turkey beak from the Turkey Strut game.

- Recruit someone to be the turkey for Dressing the Turkey.

- Acquire child's storybook about thankfulness or about the first Thanksgiving.

- Prepare refreshments. Wait until you are ready for the children to eat them before you set them out.

Group Starters

After the children have registered and received nametags, escort them to the main activity room. Invite them to guess the number of Mini Turkey Eggs in the jar. Take them to the crafts table, where they are to make handprints on construction paper. Have children put their name on their handprint. Set these aside for use later. If you anticipate a good bit of time elapsing between the first and last arrivals, set up more theme-related crafts for the children to do as they arrive, or get them involved in a game of "Turkey Says," a variation of "Simon Says." Program for maximum fun and involvement right from the start of your event.

Mixers

Pass the Drumstick

Once everyone has arrived, arrange the group in a circle, standing. Team Coaches and other adult leaders should stand in the circle as well. Introduce yourself and your program. Pass a plastic toy drumstick (or rubber chicken or plastic turkey) around the circle, having each person say her name and a favorite Thanksgiving Day food.

Variations of Pass the Drumstick

To continue warming up the group, play variations of Pass the Drumstick. Have the group pass the drumstick around the circle quickly, behind their backs, or between their legs.

Musical Drumsticks

To divide the children into teams, hand out drumsticks to as many children as you want teams. (Have each drumstick marked with a different color.) Play a lively tune, and have the children pass the drumsticks. When the music stops, the children holding the drumsticks line up with their appropriate team coach. Continue playing until all the children have gotten moved into teams. (Leaders may need to urge players to continue passing the drumsticks.)

Team Games

Pass the Corn Relay

With teams lined up relay style, give the first person in each line an ear of corn. On "go" have them pass the corn person to person to the end of the line. When the last person gets the corn, he runs to the front of the line, and passes it back. Play continues until the original first person is at the front of the line, corn in hand.

Feed the Turkeys Relay

In turn, each team member runs to a "feed bucket" approximately 15 feet away, gets five peanuts, races to the end line (an additional 15 feet away), and tries to toss the peanuts into the "feed trough" box. The player then runs straight back to the team, and tags off the next runner. Award a prize for the fastest team, as well as for the team with the most feed in their trough.

Turkey Trot Relay

In turn, each person dons a cardboard turkey beak and a belt of tail feathers, struts to the end line (approximately 25 feet away), and back gobbling like a turkey the whole way! (Be sure to give a bonus to the individuals or teams that do an especially good job strutting and gobbling!)

Pluck the Turkey

Teammates take turns running up to the poster of the turkey, plucking a feather, and returning to tag the next player. The race continues until every person has a feather for the next game.

Team Pin the Tail on the Turkey

Have teams line up shortest to tallest. In each round, a representative from each team tries to place a feather closest to the mark while blindfolded. Feathers are removed after each round. Award points to the winning team each round.

Group Games

Turkeys and Foxes (aka, Sharks and Minnows)

Designate an area with boundaries as the playing area. Start with one fox in the center. On "go" turkeys try to run across the playing area without being caught. If tagged, they become foxes also. When one turkey remains, she becomes starting fox for the next round.

Dressing the Turkey

One leader or assistant "dresses" as a turkey (in a trash bag, as described on p. 168). Issue one or two feathers with masking tape tabs to each child. Kids try to adhere their paper feathers to the turkey, while the turkey tries to avoid being taped. Use the same boundaries as in the previous game. This activity provides lots of laughs for players and spectators alike. Be sure to select an animated "turkey" who can provide the right balance between challenge and success, yet is able to keep from plowing over the smaller players.

Cool Down

Seat children on the floor. Read a story or book having to do with being thankful for all that we have and all that we are.

Thankful Feathers

Hand out the construction paper hands that the children made at the beginning of the program. Have each on write something he is thankful for on the construction paper hand. When everyone is ready, take turns reading the comments, and placing the hands on the turkey poster.

Closing

Award an appropriate prize to the winner of the Guess the Number of Mini Turkey Eggs in the jar. Award a small prize to the winning team. Distribute snack to the participants. Snack suggestions: chicken nuggets, "straw" (french fries), popcorn, mini turkey eggs, turkey or egg shaped cookies or crackers.

Thank you and good night!

Veggie Night

Parents are always telling kids, "eat your vegetables" and "don't play with your food." For all the frustrated kids out there who have ever wanted to play with their vegetables instead of eating them, this game night is for you!

Getting Ready

- Due to the amounts of fresh vegetables needed as props for this program, I recommended you run this one in the summer or around harvest time, when fresh vegetables are readily available at reasonable prices, or may be easily donated to you.

- This program is a messy one. Consider holding it out-of-doors, or in an area where you can easily clean the floor. Depending on the particular activities you choose to include, there *will* be a mess!

- Set up a sound system or boom box with some rumba-style music.

- Appropriate an assortment of obscure vegetables. Set them out on a table and label them A, B, C, D, E, etc. Lesser known vegetables such as jicama, rutabaga, turnips, or rhubarb may be good choices.

- Provide paper and pencils for participants to write down their guesses.

- Count beans (whole or dried) and place in a jar. Set jar on a table with paper and pencil for participants to write their guesses of how many beans are in the jar.

- Secure several vegetable related prizes for the Veggie ID and Bean Poll games, as well as prizes for the winning team.

- Lay out Cabbage Bowling alley with masking tape. Place six empty catsup and mustard squirt bottles on one end for pins. Get a small head of cabbage to use as the ball. If desired, make an alleyway out of a refrigerator box. Cut the box in half lengthwise, and tape the two troughs together to contain the rolling cabbage.

- Clean a long stalk of celery. Have an extra or two on hand.

- Lay out a tray of vegetables, with as many different types as you want teams. Have enough pieces of each type as you want players on the teams. Use easy to grab foods such as celery sticks, baby carrots, cucumber spears, and cherry tomatoes.

- Create a clock that looks like a beet, by drawing a large beet on a piece of posterboard or foam board. Make a "hand" for the clock, and secure it to the clock in such a way as to allow it freedom to spin. (It will need to be turned manually, unless you actually have access to a large secondhand clock like swimming teams use. In that case, carefully adhere an image of a beet to the face of the existing clock.)

- Appoint someone to manually move the hand on the beet clock during the "Beet the Clock" set of games. This person will need a digital watch or a watch with a second hand to time the events.

- Set out a card table for each team, or have two teams share a longer table. Tables should be covered with paper or vinyl tablecloths.

- Recruit someone with a secondhand watch or stopwatch to time events.

- Get a dozen ears of corn for each team. Keep the husks on! Also give each team a bag for collecting husks and a bag or pot for collecting husked corn.

- Purchase enough fresh green beans for each team to have about 50. Make sure each team has the same number of green beans. Place each team's beans in a bag and have a bowl for each team in which they can put their cleaned beans.

- Secure a large number of fresh peas, still in the pod. Each team should have the same number of pea pods, and a bowl for the hulled peas.

- Get a medium to large onion per team, and put each one in a separate plastic bag. Each team will also need a pair of latex gloves and a pair of safety goggles. Leader will need a sharp knife.

- Prepare two-feet lengths of quarter-inch dowel to be pool cues. Sandpaper the ends to make them smooth, or locate miniature pool cues from a child's game. Each team needs a cue, and a 9- to 16-ounce size paper cup with masking tape.

- Purchase medium-sized, ripe tomatoes, enough for half of your participants, plus a few extras.

- Have inexpensive, large-sized trash bag liners available for participants who would like to use them as a cover-up.

- Each team will need a bandana, cowboy hat, pair of safety goggles, a "holster" of some sort, and 10 to 12 pieces of raw okra.

- Gather supplies needed for Tossing a Salad event. Each team will need a chef's hat, cover-up, safety goggles, a large mixing bowl (stainless steel, industrial size would be ideal), plastic pancake turner, head of lettuce (cut into eight to ten wedges), one quarter head of red cabbage (shredded), two carrots (cut into coins), four radishes (sliced), large tomato (cut into thin wedges), one cucumber (sliced), two water pistols (one filled with water—we'll call it clear oil—the other with vinegar).

Group Starters

Strange Veggie ID

Set out and number various bizarre vegetables. Have paper and pencils available to participants and encourage early arrivals submit a guess for each vegetable.

The Bean Poll

Guess the number of beans (peas, button mushrooms) in the jar.

Cabbage Bowling

Set up a bowling alley with empty catsup and mustard squirt bottles as pins. Players roll heads of cabbage to try to knock down pins.

Mixers

As you welcome your group, be sure to introduce your MC (Mustard of Ceremonies), Artie Choke, and his Lovely Assistant, The Radishing Beauty, Sally Dressing.

Rutabaga Rumba

At the beginning of the program, rumba music is played, and participants and spectators are instructed to do the "Rutabaga Rumba" every time the music is played. (Any type of wiggly dance will suffice!) Music should be played periodically, particularly during down times between events.

The Celery Stalk

A tag game, where "It" has a stalk of celery, and uses it to gently whack a person to tag them. Once someone is tagged, they take the piece of celery and begin "stalking" their next victim.

Team Dividing

Determine the number of teams you want, and set out enough vegetable strips for each participant to have one. For instance, to divide the group into two teams of 12 players on each team, lay out 12 baby carrots and 12 celery sticks on a tray. Instruct players to run to the tray, retrieve one vegetable strip, and then return to the starting line—without eating their vegetable! After participants have all returned to the starting area, have them race to locate their other teammates. Once found, the teams should sit in a circle and consume their vegetable sticks. As soon as their vegetables are swallowed, players should begin chanting their vegetable/team name: Carrots! Carrots! until everyone on their team has joined in the cheer. The first team to totally consume their vegetables and have everyone seated and chanting wins 200 cucumber chips (aka, points) for their team.

Beet the Clock

The following five fast-paced activities will be done against the clock. The winning team receives 500 cucumber chips (aka, points) for their team.

Corn Husking for Speed

Each team gets a dozen ears of corn, which they must completely husk.

Snap Beans

Each team given equal number of beans. They must snap both ends off, and place in a bowl.

Hulling Peas

Each team gets same number of peas and must remove them from the pods.

Mind Your Peas and Cues

Contestants use miniature pool cues (from child's game, or quarter-inch dowels in two-feet lengths) to knock fresh or frozen peas across the width of a table into a paper cup "pocket" taped to the side. Players take turns, each contestant getting 15 to 20 seconds to try to pocket as many peas as possible.

Onion Peeling

Each team sends a representative who gets an onion of approximately the same size. The top half inch is sliced off, and players must race to pull off each layer. Each layer must be removed individually.

"Peared" Events

Tomato Toss

Have teammates partner up, and form two lines, with pairs standing opposite one another. As in the familiar egg toss game, players in one line are given a ripe tomato. On the "Ready, Toss" signal, these players toss their tomato to their partners, and take a giant step backwards. On the "Ready, Toss" signal, these partners toss the tomatoes back, and step backwards themselves. Players continue to toss and move back on signal until only one pair remains with an unsmashed tomato. (Advise players to dress in old clothes, or issue trash bag liner "cover ups" to players.)

Shoot Out at the Okra Corral

Each team sends a representative to participate in the shoot out. Give opponents bandanas, cowboy hats, and safety goggles, and a holster full of raw okra. Start with players standing back to back, then have them take five paces, turn and start firing okra at the other. Object is to hit your opponent, while dodging the shots he's taking at you! (If there appears to be an excellent "marksman" among the contestants, award extra points to that team. Give all others 500 "cucumber chips" for their effort.)

Featured Activity

Leaders: This extremely messy activity is best done outdoors!

Tossing a Salad

Players from each team compete, racing against other teams and the clock. One person (the Master Salad Chef) stands 15–20 feet away from her teammates, wearing a chef's hat, cover-up, and safety goggles, and holding a large mixing bowl. The other teammates stand at their team's table, which holds the salad ingredients, and a large, plastic pancake turner to help guide and catch as much salad as possible. Salad ingredients (listed in the Getting Ready section above), should be distributed to each team, placed on their table. Each team should also have a squirt gun of "oil" and one of vinegar. From this table, team players load ingredients onto a pancake turner and catapult them into the salad bowl. The team's Chef, holding the salad bowl, may move within a designated area to try to catch as much salad as possible. Once all the salad ingredients have been catapulted, players try to squirt as much "oil" and vinegar into the bowl as possible.

Teams have 60 seconds to toss as much salad as possible. The team with the most salad in their bowl wins 2000 cucumber chips! The other team(s) have to help clean up the mess!

Cool Down

Once you've got the mess cleaned up a little, and you've settled the victors down, assemble the entire group in a seated circle. Now it is time to gather together to enjoy your own spontaneous rendition of "All My Veggies: An Ongoing Veggie Tale of Triumph and Tragedy." Drawing upon the characters on the Veggie Tales videos, the Leader begins with a general opening statement, such as, "Once upon a time, there was a lonely cucumber named Larry." The person next to her picks up the story, beginning his one sentence contribution with the word, "Fortunately..." The next person in the circle continues the story, beginning her sentence with "Unfortunately..." And so the story of vegetable intrigue continues, alternating Fortunately/Unfortunately openers. When it becomes the leader's turn again, she brings the story to a quick conclusion—or leaves the story hanging "To Be Continued..."

> **Note:** It is important to wash vegetables before consuming them. Similarly, encourage story contributors to "keep the veggies clean"—for general consumption!

Award prizes for Group Starter activities and team prizes. Serve refreshments, such as veggies and dip, carrot cake, potato chips, zucchini bread, popcorn, or corn on the cob.

Winter Wackyland

Kids of all ages will enjoy getting into the holiday spirit with this program. It's just the right mix of festive and frivolous fanatical fun.

Getting Ready

- Deck the halls (walls, windows, tables, and doors) with boughs of holly, pine, garland, and colored lights. The more decorations the better.

- Prepare red slips of paper with stars on them, enough for each person to get one. One of the stars should be a different color than the others.

- Find small prizes for Secret Star and Santa's Helper game.

- Provide a four-inch by six-inch note card and pencil for each player.

- Ready large pile of miscellaneous clothes and household items for Shop Til You Drop.

- Ready color-coordinated tags, at least five per color. Each team will be assigned a different color. Safety pin tags to different items, making sure each team has the same number of items tagged.

- Locate several shopping bags with handles, one large one per team.

- Prepare a large number of wrapped "gifts" and gift bags for Christmas Shopping Shuffle. (Use empty cereal, tissue, and cake mix boxes, or whatever is readily available.) Each team needs the same number of items.

- For each team, gather a very large jacket and pair of pants, a hat, pair of mittens, a scarf, and a shopping sack.

- Arrange a large square of chairs, so each side has enough chairs for every team member. (Each side of the square will accommodate a team.)

- Locate a large cup, mug, or handled mixing bowl for each team.

- Purchase enough large marshmallows for each person to have four, plus several extra bags of marshmallows for the Snow Ball Fight.

- Borrow or purchase extra large, V-neck shirts, one for each team.

- Get a marshmallow Santa or similar prize for the winner of Frosty, the Marshmallow Man.

- Mark out two adjacent large squares on the floor with masking tape. Determine size of the squares by the number of players you have.

- Locate two grocery store paper bags for the Snow Ball Fight.

- Assemble props needed for each team for Mama's Medicine: chair, bib, large serving spoon, large amber-colored medicine bottle, strawberry milkshake.

- Prize for each "patient" (perhaps a roll of antacid!) and for the winner of Mama's Medicine.

- Have a little prize to give the winning team.

Mixers

Secret Star

Here's a holiday way to get your group started. Give each person a little piece of red paper with a star on it. Pieces should be small enough to fit easily in the palm of their hands. Players mingle around the room, approaching other players with a "Ho Ho Ho." The person that is approached holds out both clenched fists, and asks, "Right or left?" The other player guesses one, and that hand is opened. If the star is in that hand, the player who correctly guessed it may take it. If he guessed incorrectly, the star remains with its owner. No one may approach the same person twice in a row. He may come back to the first person after challenging another player. Even if you lose your star, you may continue to challenge people. If a player has accumulated several stars, they are all put in the fist. When a player loses his star, he loses all of them.

Oh, yes. There is one star that is a different color. Whoever has that star at the end of the five-minute playing period wins a prize. (P.S. No fair sticking the "Secret Star" in your pocket until the game ends!)

Santa's Helpers

Santa had made a list, and was about to check it for the second time when his computer when down! He needs help from the group to gather information about what people want for Christmas. To do this, give every person a sheet of paper and a pencil. On the "go" signal players try to make a list of what others want by approaching someone and saying, "Ho Ho Ho! What would you like for Christmas?" This person tells "Santa" his or her name, plus something he'd like for Christmas (real or outrageous!). "Santa" writes the information down and heads off to ask someone else, or to be asked by someone else. Allow players five minutes, then award a prize to the person with the most names on their paper.

Ha Ha Hee Hee Ho Ho Song

What better way to get in the holiday mood than with a little "Jingle Bells." Sing the first verse, and after going through the chorus one time to refamiliarize everyone, divide the group into thirds based on where they are sitting or standing. Start the song again, and this time, instead of singing the opening words of the chorus, one third sings "Ha-Ha-Ha" instead of "Jin-gle-Bells," the second third sings "Hee-Hee-Hee" instead of the second "Jin-gle-Bells," and the remaining group sings "Ho-Ho-Ho-Ho-Ho" instead of "Jin-gle-all-the-way" when the song leader points to them. Various parts of the song can have "Ha's," "Hee's," and "Ho's" inserted at the whim of the leader's pointing finger.

Team Events

To divide the group into teams, have participants look at their name tags. Each should have a holiday symbol on it: Christmas tree, Santa, Snowman, Reindeer. On the "go" signal everyone begins singing the song that corresponds to their symbol, as a means of locating their teams. Those with Christmas trees sing "O, Christmas Tree." Those with Santas sing "Santa Claus Is Coming to Town." Those with snowmen sing "Frosty, the Snowman." Those with reindeer sing "Rudolph, the Red-Nosed Reindeer." Be sure to sing the first line of each song as you give the directions, so everyone becomes familiar with their tune.

Shop Til You Drop

Place a large pile of miscellaneous clothing and household items on a table. Ahead of time, saftey-pin color-coordinated tags onto some of the items, so each racer will be able to collect one of the tagged items. Assign each team one of the colors of the tags. Each team supplies five players (and that number may vary depending on how much stuff you want the team to accumulate). The first player from each team is given a shopping bag, and is shown the type of tag that their team is trying to locate. On the "go" signal, the first player from each team runs up to the pile and begins rummaging through, to locate an item with the correct tag on it. After she locates one item, she stuffs it into the bag, returns to her team, and hands the shopping bag to the next player in line. So the game continues until one team has located all the items with their tags on them. Points of Rummage Etiquette: (1) Items must be kept on the table, and (2) It ain't nice to swipe items containing tags belonging to other teams!

Christmas Shopping Shuffle

Prepare an equal number of wrapped gifts or gift bags for each team, and place a stack opposite each team, at a distance of 40 to 50 feet. On the "go" signal the first person from each team races up and grabs a gift—any gift—and hands it to the second person in line. Keeping a hold of that gift, the second person races up to her team's stack, and grabs a second gift. She passes them both to the third player, who keeps those gifts, and gathers another. And so the race goes, with each person racing with one more package than the person before them. Makes for some hilarious, harried shopping!

Bundle Up Relay

Here's a game you'll want to play before heading out into the blizzardy winter weather. Each team needs a jacket, pair of pants (oversized, of course!), a hat, pair of mittens, a scarf, and a shopping sack. (You may want to have these articles of clothing be the items the team collects in the Shop Til You Drop game.) Have each team sit in a row of chairs side-by-side. Arrange teams so they can see each other. The first person on each team is given the selected items. On the "go" signal the first person "dresses," grabs the shopping bag, and races around the front of the team, then around behind the team, and returns to his original chair. He "unbundles," and hands everything to the player seated next to him, who puts it all on, and races around the team. (Yes, it is OK for teammates to assist.) First team to complete this fiasco, and return all the items to the bag wins!

Swiss Hit or Miss

Everyone knows nothing calms a harried shopper like a cup of hot cocoa—especially if it has marshmallows in it. And the more marshmallows the better! In the center of the area where the teams' chairs are arranged, place a *large* cup or mug for each team (handled mixing bowls work great). Give each player four marshmallows. On the signal, players try to toss as many marshmallows into their team's cup as possible. After everyone has tossed them, count up how many there are in each cup. If your marshmallow lands in another team's cup, well, just consider it a gift to them.

The Making of Frosty, the Marshmallow Man

Redistribute the marshmallows from the previous game, so each player again has four. This time, get a volunteer from each team who is willing to be transformed into Frosty, the Marshmallow Man. Have this person put on a V-neck shirt on over his own shirt, and tuck it in at the bottom. Standing in front of his team, the volunteer holds open the top of his shirt, so his teammates can toss in as many marshmallows as they can. Tossers must remain seated, and may not pick up any marshmallows from the floor to toss. Once the marshmallows have all been tossed, have a teammate help count up the number of marshmallows that made it into the shirt, and see who was the champion Frosty, the Marshmallow Man. Award some appropriate prize— like a bag of marshmallows!

Featured Activities

Snow Ball Fight

Having just tossed around marshmallows, it is difficult for even the most orderly group to refrain from taking pop shots at one another. So...Designate an area for a Snow Ball Fight! Mark a center line on the floor, using masking tape. Give each team 40 large marshmallows (a 10-ounce bag). Pile them near the center line, yell "Go!" and stand back! After 30 seconds, whistle for "Stop!" Hand each team a grocery bag, and have them count the marshmallows as they place them in the bag. The team with the lower number wins the round, as they were quicker at unloading their arsenal on the other team. Play several rounds, keeping score after each round. The winning team could have snack first, or win a prize, or just have the satisfaction that they are the champion snow ball fighters!

Mama's Medicine

The only bad part about the holiday season is that all that running around shopping, snow ball fighting, bundling up, and unbundling can sometimes get a body sick. Good thing Mama's got some of that great pink gooey medicine.

Get two volunteers from each team: one to be the "Mother" and one to be the "Patient." Sit the patients in chairs, and put bibs on them. Hand the mothers large serving spoons, and large medicine bottles filled with strawberry milkshake. Make sure everyone knows it's actually a strawberry milkshake, not real medicine! On the "go" signal the mothers feed the patients their "medicine" until the complete dose (a predetermined amount based on bottle size) has been consumed. Be sure to award these good sports with praise and a prize.

Cool Down

- Award team prizes.

- Have everyone sing "We Wish You a Merry Christmas" (or some other simple holiday song), then direct them to enjoy some holiday snacks such as eggnog, hot cocoa, or warmed cider.

- Thank everyone (participants and leadership team alike) for helping to get us all in the holiday spirit!

Concluding Thoughts...

Now that you've had a chance to look at the themed special events in this book, I hope you're as excited as I am to get started facilitating fun for folks! People really love the opportunity to get out and have some wholesome fun and excitement in their lives, and you are just the person to make it possible for them. Through these themed special events, you can lift people's spirits, remind them they are valuable members of society (and their team), and let them know they can enjoy the company of others—while being slightly crazy!

Keep in mind the main purpose of these programs is to build people up. As you select activities and as you lead them, please be mindful of this. Physical and emotional safety is important. All that we say and do through these events should have a positive impact on every person who attends.

Your efforts in creating and delivering great themed special events like the ones here in *Boredom Busters* will be appreciated far beyond your imagination. Kids who never get picked for a team will feel included and important as they first realize they are making great contributions to their group and having a great time in the process. Parents who may have fallen into the rut of seeing their child as "not as good" as others start beaming with pride as their young one races off to victory during one of your relay races. Even older adults who wonder if they are still needed and valued by the community are reassured when they score points for their team by knowing the answer to a trivia question or by being an encouragement to others. Family ties will be strengthened, individuals built up, and memories made—all because of the investments you will be making in the lives of others.

We are a very wealthy society, where so many have so much. Yet regardless of one's social status, we all yearn to be valued by others, to know we are able to contribute to something bigger than ourselves, and to have a little excitement in our lives. I know we can't solve all the problems of the world through themed special events like these, but every positive investment in others contributes to our common good.

You are about to undertake a noble and meaningful task. You and I both know how much planning and preparation go into these events. Never forget that it's worth the effort. I encourage you to gather a team of assistants around you, select a themed special event you'd like to try, and get going. Celebrate each opportunity you have to touch people's lives in a positive way, and remember to thank them for allowing you to do so.

I wish I could be there to watch you shine as you lead others in joyous activities designed to delight their hearts and encourage their lives. I know you'll do a great job and will be an incredible blessing to all those who will attend.

Let the fun begin!

Other Books by Venture Publishing

21st Century Leisure: Current Issues, Second Edition
by Valeria J. Freysinger and John R. Kelly

The A•B•Cs of Behavior Change: Skills for Working With Behavior Problems in Nursing Homes
by Margaret D. Cohn, Michael A. Smyer, and Ann L. Horgas

Activity Experiences and Programming within Long-Term Care
by Ted Tedrick and Elaine R. Green

The Activity Gourmet
by Peggy Powers

Advanced Concepts for Geriatric Nursing Assistants
by Carolyn A. McDonald

Adventure Programming
edited by John C. Miles and Simon Priest

Assessment: The Cornerstone of Activity Programs
by Ruth Perschbacher

Behavior Modification in Therapeutic Recreation: An Introductory Manual
by John Dattilo and William D. Murphy

Benefits of Leisure
edited by B. L. Driver, Perry J. Brown, and George L. Peterson

Benefits of Recreation Research Update
by Judy M. Sefton and W. Kerry Mummery

Beyond Baskets and Beads: Activities for Older Adults With Functional Impairments
by Mary Hart, Karen Primm, and Kathy Cranisky

Beyond Bingo: Innovative Programs for the New Senior
by Sal Arrigo, Jr., Ann Lewis, and Hank Mattimore

Beyond Bingo 2: More Innovative Programs for the New Senior
by Sal Arrigo, Jr.

Both Gains and Gaps: Feminist Perspectives on Women's Leisure
by Karla Henderson, M. Deborah Bialeschki, Susan M. Shaw, and Valeria J. Freysinger

Client Assessment in Therapeutic Recreation Services
by Norma J. Stumbo

Client Outcomes in Therapeutic Recreation Services
edited by Norma J. Stumbo

Conceptual Foundations for Therapeutic Recreation
edited by David R. Austin, John Dattilo, and Bryan P. McCormick

Dimensions of Choice: A Qualitative Approach to Recreation, Parks, and Leisure Research
by Karla A. Henderson

Dementia Care Programming: An Identity-Focused Approach
By Rosemary Dunne

Diversity and the Recreation Profession: Organizational Perspectives
edited by Maria T. Allison and Ingrid E. Schneider

Effective Management in Therapeutic Recreation Service
by Gerald S. O'Morrow and Marcia Jean Carter

Evaluating Leisure Services: Making Enlightened Decisions, Second Edition
by Karla A. Henderson and M. Deborah Bialeschki

Everything From A to Y: The Zest Is up to You! Older Adult Activities for Every Day of the Year
by Nancy R. Cheshire and Martha L. Kenney

Leadership and Administration of Outdoor Pursuits, Second Edition
by Phyllis Ford and James Blanchard

Leadership in Leisure Services: Making a Difference, Second Edition
by Debra J. Jordan

Leisure and Leisure Services in the 21st Century
by Geoffrey Godbey

The Leisure Diagnostic Battery: Users Manual and Sample Forms
by Peter A. Witt and Gary Ellis

Leisure Education I: A Manual of Activities and Resources, Second Edition
by Norma J. Stumbo

Leisure Education II: More Activities and Resources, Second Edition
by Norma J. Stumbo

Leisure Education III: More Goal-Oriented Activities
by Norma J. Stumbo

Leisure Education IV: Activities for Individuals with Substance Addictions
by Norma J. Stumbo

Leisure Education Program Planning: A Systematic Approach, Second Edition
by John Dattilo

Leisure Education Specific Programs
by John Dattilo

Leisure in Your Life: An Exploration, Sixth Edition
by Geoffrey Godbey

Leisure Services in Canada: An Introduction, Second Edition
by Mark S. Searle and Russell E. Brayley

Leisure Studies: Prospects for the Twenty-First Century
edited by Edgar L. Jackson and Thomas L. Burton

The Lifestory Re-Play Circle: A Manual of Activities and Techniques
by Rosilyn Wilder

The Melody Lingers On: A Complete Music Activities Program for Older Adults
by Bill Messenger

Models of Change in Municipal Parks and Recreation: A Book of Innovative Case Studies
edited by Mark E. Havitz

More Than a Game: A New Focus on Senior Activity Services
by Brenda Corbett

Nature and the Human Spirit: Toward an Expanded Land Management Ethic
edited by B. L. Driver, Daniel Dustin, Tony Baltic, Gary Elsner, and George Peterson

The Organizational Basis of Leisure Participation: A Motivational Exploration
by Robert A. Stebbins

Outdoor Recreation for 21st Century America
by H. Ken Cordell, principal author

Outdoor Recreation Management: Theory and Application, Third Edition
by Alan Jubenville and Ben Twight

Planning Parks for People, Second Edition
by John Hultsman, Richard L. Cottrell, and Wendy Z. Hultsman

The Process of Recreation Programming Theory and Technique, Third Edition
by Patricia Farrell and Herberta M. Lundegren

Programming for Parks, Recreation, and Leisure Services: A Servant Leadership Approach
by Donald G. DeGraaf, Debra J. Jordan, and Kathy H. DeGraaf